HEWLETT-PACKARD LASER PRINTER POWER PACK

HEWLETT-PACKARD LASER PRINTER POWER PACK

Includes Laser-ToolKit™ Utility Diskette

Peter G. Randall
and
Steven J. Bennett

A Brady Utility

New York London Toronto Sydney Tokyo Singapore

Brady

Simon & Schuster, Inc.
Gulf + Western Building
One Gulf + Western Plaza
New York, NY 10023

DISTRIBUTED BY PRENTICE HALL TRADE

Manufactured in the United States of America

2 3 4 5 6 7 8 9 10

Library of Congress Cataloging-in-Publication Data

Randall, Peter G., 1951–
Hewlett-Packard laser printer power pack [computer file].

1 computer disk ; 5¼ in. + 1 v.
System requirements: IBM PC, XT, AT, PS/2, or
100% compatible computer; 256K; DOS 2.1 or MS-DOS 2.0;
2 disk drives or 1 hard disk; monochrome monitor;
Hewlett-Packard or 100% compatible laser printer.
Title from title screen.

"Brady utility software."
Audience: Adult microcomputer users.
Summary: A utility containing macros, batch files,
command functions, and printer control functions for
use in creating professional-quality documents on a
HP laser printer easily. Contains programs and macros
for Lotus 1-2-3 (Release 2/2.01), dBase III Plus, and
WordPerfect (Version 4.2), and BASIC. Includes PCL printer language
coverage.
1. Utilities (Computer programs)--Software.
I. Bennett, Steven J., 1951– , II. Lotus 1-2-3.
(Computer program) III. dBase III plus (Computer
program) IV. WordPerfect (Computer program)
QA76.76.U84R36 1988 004.7′7 88-8663
ISBN 0-13-387705-1

CONTENTS

Limits of Liability and Disclaimer of Warranty

The author and publisher of this book have used their best efforts in preparing this book and the programs contained in it. These efforts include the development, research, and testing of the theories and programs to determine their effectiveness. The author and publisher make no warranty of any kind, expressed or implied, with regard to these programs or the documentation contained in this book. The author and publisher shall not be liable in any event for incidental or consequential damages in connection with, or arising out of, the furnishing, performance, or use of these programs.

Registered Trademarks

dBASE III Plus is a registered trademark of Ashton-Tate.

IBM is a registered trademark of International Business Machines Corporation.

IBM PC, XT, AT, and PS/12 are registered trademarks of the International Business Machines Corporation.

Helvetica is a trademark of Linotype.

Hewlett-Packard and LaserJet are registered trademarks of Hewlett-Packard Company.

Lotus 1-2-3 is a registered trademark of Lotus Development Corp.

Microsoft Word is a registered trademark of Microsoft Corporation.

PostScript is a registered trademark of Adobe Systems Inc.

Times is a trademark of Linotype.

WordPerfect is registered trademark of WordPerfect, Inc.

FOREWORD

HP's LaserJet Printers have been in the office for five years now, revolutionizing the way we communicate in the business world. Now, anyone can tap the power of the LaserJet printer and create exquisite pages, with a typeset look and feel. HP has worked closely with software vendors to ensure good software support for the LaserJet printer family. Today, LaserJet printer drivers are standard in the most popular PC software packages, making it easier for anyone to take advantage of the LaserJet's remarkable capabilities to merge text and graphics, and print a wide variety of fonts on a single page.

Still, there are some software packages that provide limited support for laser printers, requiring the user to delve into what may at first seem like an intimidating world of printer language programming. This book-diskette kit makes it easy to use HP's LaserJet PCL primer language codes to create just the look you're seeking. Authors Peter Randall and Steve Bennett have created an in-depth course in PCL programming. They've also included a series of software application hints that will help you use your LaserJet printer more effectively with a variety of packages.

The diskette included with this book is a useful utility for the LaserJet user. Just load the diskette on your PC, and you'll find a broad selection of programs and macros for Lotus 1-2-3, dBASE and WordPerfect. There's even a menu for all of the major font cartridges, so you can easily select fonts to use with any software package.

Whatever your level of expertise with the LaserJet, you'll find this book/disk kit a valuable addition to your library. It is useful for novices and experts alike—there's something worthwhile in it for every member of the LaserJet printer family.

William P. McGlynn
Marketing Manager,
Hewlett-Packard, Boise Printer Division

ACKNOWLEDGMENTS

This book couldn't have happened without the many hours that the staff of Hewlett-Packard's Boise, Idaho division spent with us explaining concepts, sharing information, and reviewing manuscript. First, thanks to Jeri Peterson, Director of Public Relations at HP Boise, for coordinating our project with the technical support staff. We'd like to express our deepest appreciation to Walt Sledzieski, Manager of Support Services, for the hours he put into the project—Walt not only served as general information source, but he read through our manuscript dotting every "i" and crossing every "t." Thanks, too, go to Thad Webster for boosting our understanding of PCL. In addition, we'd like to acknowledge the contribution of Judy Ross and Sue Despot, who promptly sent us literature and materials as we needed them.

At Simon & Schuster, our editor, Milissa Koloski, provided an excellent sense of direction and helped us conceptualize the project from the beginning. As usual, she was an important member of our team. We'd also like to thank Michael Mellin, associate publisher, who believed in this project from the start and offered his support and enthusiasm while we completed it. Finally, Michael Cooper is to be congratulated for his magnificent handling of a challenging production job.

QUICK START FOR THE LASER-TOOLKIT UTILITY DISKETTE

The diskette enclosed in the back cover of this book contains 100 files for increasing your productivity with a Hewlett-Packard LaserJet, LaserJet PLUS, LaserJet 500 Plus, LaserJet Series II, LaserJet 2000, or compatible printer. If you want to leap in and use the utilities, please read the following. Even if you're an experienced user, we recommend that you first skim the Laser-ToolKit documentation (pages 1 to 43)—you'll find complete information about the utilities and how to best use them.

Backing Up the Utility Diskette

The Laser-ToolKit Utility Disk is not copy protected. Make a backup copy of the diskette immediately. Use the DOS DISKCOPY command to copy all files and subdirectories to a blank diskette. Please note that the Utility Disk contains a number of subdirectories which in turn contain many individual files. The DISKCOPY command will recreate the necessary subdirectories on the backup diskette, while the DOS COPY command will not.

Installing the Programs

dBASE and WordPerfect Utility Programs

To use any of the Laser-ToolKit utility programs contained in the root directory of the diskette, simply copy the programs to your current directory or diskette. Please note that several of the dBASE programs, as well as several of the WordPerfect macros, work together and must all be present in the current directory or diskette to operate correctly. Check the individual application notes in this section for the lists of file names associated with each application.

Lotus 1-2-3 Utilities

The Lotus 1-2-3 macros are all contained in a single file called 123MACRO.WK1. You must first copy the file to the current directory or diskette and then you must copy the individual macros from the 123MACRO worksheet to your own worksheet using the 1-2-3 command /**F**ile **C**ombine **C**opy **N**amed range. Finally you must name the macro and name the individual range names in the macro. See the 123MACRO application notes (page 24) for detailed instructions for the naming procedures.

BASIC Files Containing PCL Commands

Many of the BASIC files have a corresponding BATCH that executes it. The BASIC and BATCH files are contained in individual subdirectories corresponding to each of the font cartridges. This allows you to quickly copy all the files for a particular cartridge to your current directory or diskette. The DOS command for copying the files for the Hewlett-Packard *Z* cartridge residing in the CART-Z subdirectory is as follows:

```
COPY a:\CART-Z\*.*
[target directory or diskette]
```

where the target directory or diskette represents the name of the directory or diskette drive to which you wish to copy the files.

BASIC programs have been included for the HP *A, B, C, F, G, H, J, L, M, N, R, T, Y,* and *Z* cartridges. You'll also find BASIC programs for the JetWare JetFont 123 cartridge from Computer Peripherals Inc. The JetWare cartridge files are in a directory called Lotica.

SYSTEM REQUIREMENTS FOR USING THE LASER-TOOLKIT

1. IBM PC/XT/AT/PS/2 or 100 percent compatible
2. Sufficient RAM for your application programs
3. DOS version required by your software and/or hardware LaserJet, LaserJet PLUS, LaserJet 500, LaserJet Series II, LaserJet 2000, or laser printer that emulates Hewlett-Packard's Printer Command Language (PCL)

INTRODUCTION

When Hewlett-Packard introduced the LaserJet in 1984, it did not anticipate starting a revolution in the office place. Yet the printer took off beyond anyone's wildest dreams. And, in retrospect, it makes perfectly good sense. The LaserJet is extremely fast, quiet, runs on cut sheet paper rather than pinfeed stock, offers excellent resolution and a wide variety of fonts, and can mix text and graphics on a single page.

Despite the widespread acceptance of the LaserJet and compatibles, most laser printers are only used as fast line printers, with one or two fonts. While more and more software vendors are supplying drivers for the LaserJet, making it easy to access various fonts, the majority of software available today is still written for dot matrix printers or daisy wheel printers, and in many situations, you're on your own if you want to do anything but print in the default Courier typeface. That means instructing with complex *Printer Command Language* (PCL) codes. For example, if you wanted to use the Times Roman, 10-point bold font on the popular *F* cartridge, and your software did not provide explicit commands for that font, you would need to write the following BASIC program:

```
100 LPRINT CHR$(027);"&l0O";
200 LPRINT CHR$(027);"(8U";
300 LPRINT CHR$(027);"(s1p10v0s3b5T"
```

and run it before starting your application program.

You probably have better things to do than write BASIC programs just to run your printer. That's why we wrote this book/diskette "tool kit." The diskette enclosed in the back cover contains professionally written and debugged BASIC programs for the most popular HP cartridges: *A, B, C, F, G, H, J, L, M, N, R, T, Y,* and *Z.* In addition, the disk provides files for the JetWare JetFont 123 cartridge from Computer Peripherals Inc., which includes a 30 character per inch font that will enable you to cram 390 columns of text on a sheet of legal paper printed in Landscape orientation. Each program provides an on-screen menu with selections for all of the fonts on the associated cartridge (see Figure 0.1). To select a font, all you need to do is run the program, then choose the appropriate menu item. No fuss, no programming skills—you have instant access to your LaserJet's full power.

```
        Laser ToolKit(tm) Font Menu
              H.P. Cartridge F

  1. Courier        10  Medium  Portrait
  2. Courier        10  Medium  Landscape

  3. Times Roman     8  Medium  Portrait
  4. Times Roman    10  Medium  Portrait
  5. Times Roman    10  Bold    Portrait
  6. Times Roman    10  Italic  Portrait

  7. Helvetica      14  Bold    Portrait

  8. Line Printer 16  Medium  Portrait

         0 = Exit Without Change

             Enter Selection:
```

Figure 0.1 Sample font menu for HP F cartrirdge.

In addition to the font cartridge programs, you'll also find a number of programs for dBASE III Plus, and macros for Lotus 1-2-3 Release 2/2.01 and WordPerfect Version 4.2. These programs will help you use your LaserJet to the fullest potential with the most popular application programs.

While the programs have been specifically written for the HP LaserJet, LaserJet PLUS, LaserJet 500 PLUS, LaserJet Series II, and LaserJet 2000 printers, they can drive any laser printer that emulates the Hewlett-Packard PCL printer language. If you're not sure whether your laser printer can emulate PCL, refer to your manual or check with your dealer.

If you want to write your own programs for specialized applications, we've included the PCL primer (Section II), which provides an easy-to-follow but comprehensive crash course in using Hewlett-Packard's printer command language. Once you've read through the PCL primer, you'll be able to write your own programs from scratch, or modify the programs on the diskette. Finally, you'll find a special section with software notes and suggestions that will help you set up and use your LaserJet with Lotus 1-2-3 Release 2/2.01, WordPerfect Versions 4.2 and 5.0, and Word 4.0.

We've designed this book/diskette package to help you use your LaserJet in new and exciting ways. We recommend that you experiment with the programs, and browse through the PCL primer and software notes. You're sure to find some nuggets of information that will make your daily computing more productive, efficient, and enjoyable.

Peter G. Randall
Steven J. Bennett

I SOFTWARE DOCUMENTATION

The diskette enclosed in the back cover contains programs and macros for getting the most out of your LaserJet. The BASIC files enable you to run 12-pitch and line-printer (16.66-pitch) condensed print when using DOS, or when running application software that does not support laser printers. The dBASE programs enable you to access those fonts from within dBASE III Plus, and the Lotus 1-2-3 macros allow you to print entire spreadsheets in a selected font, or portions of a worksheet (such as column headings).

The following documentation provides you with the information you need to load and use the files and macros. You'll also find suggestions for customizing the programs and macros. We encourage you to experiment—the utilities may open a whole new world of printing for you!

GENERAL BASIC FILES

BASIC and Batch Files

Directory Location

The directory in which the files are located corresponds to the cartridge identifier letter. For example, the HP *A* cartridge is located in a directory called CART-A, while the Z cartridge is located in the directory CART-Z. You will find files for the following Hewlett-Packard font cartridges: A, B, C, F, G, H, J, L, M, N, R, T, Y, and Z. In addition, the disk has a directory called Lotica, which contains files for the JetWare JetFont 123 cartridge made by Computer Peripherals Inc.

Software Required

BASIC—Available on all IBM PC and MS-DOS machines.

Application

Selecting various fonts from the most popular font cartridges. Use the BASIC files to select fonts when running programs that do not support the LaserJet. For example, if your accounting program does not offer a compressed print setting, you could load a line printer font from DOS using one of the BASIC programs, then load your accounting module, and your reports should print in the selected line printer typeface. (Note: Some applications issue a printer reset as part of their start-up procedure, which may override your selection. You will have to experiment with each application.)

Description and Usage

The BASIC files contain PCL strings for selecting printer fonts. The batch files are used to easily execute the BASIC files. There are four types of files in each directory:

1. *The "workhorse" BASIC files used to select the designated font.* The file names correspond to the fonts they select. The first several letters describe the font face:

   TR = Times Roman

   HELV = Helvetica

   LP = Line Printer

   C = Courier

   LOT = Lotica

   The digits in the center represent the font point size: 12 = 12 point, 14 = 14 point, and so on. The first letter following the point size stands for the stroke weight:

   L = Light

   M = Medium

   B = Bold

   The last letter before the decimal point indicates the orientation:

   P = Portrait

   L = Landscape

   For example, TR12BP.BAS is the name of the BASIC file corresponding to Times Roman, 12-point, bold, Portrait font.
2. *Batch Files.* Each BATCH file executes a corresponding BASIC file, which has the same prefix. The only difference in naming is that the BATCH files have a .BAT extension, instead of .BAS for BASIC file.
3. *The menu file, "FONT-Z.BAS."* This special BASIC file displays a menu of the font choices available on the font cartridge, giving the user the ability to select the desired font by entering a single number from the menu. The last letter of the file name corresponds to the cartridge identifier, so that FONT-Z corresponds to the Z cartridge.

(LOTICA.BAS corresponds to the JetWare JetFont 123 cartridge.)

You can activate each of the BASIC programs in one of two ways:

1. You can load the BASIC program into memory, by typing BASIC at the DOS prompt. With IBM PCs, the BASIC program is stored in ROM and is always available. With some clones, you may have to load BASIC from your MS-DOS system diskette or other diskette supplied with your machine. After you have started BASIC, you must load and run the selected BASIC program. The command to load the program TR12BP.BAS is:

   ```
   LOAD"TR12BP
   ```

   and the command to run it is:

   ```
   RUN
   ```

   When the program is finished, you will be returned to DOS automatically. You can combine these steps into a single step by entering the command:

   ```
   BASIC TR12BP
   ```

   at the DOS prompt.

2. A much simpler method is to create an associated BATCH file, which loads BASIC and runs the selected BASIC program. Since they have the same prefix names as their BASIC program counterparts, you need only type the prefix, as in:

   ```
   TR12BP
   ```

   to run both the BATCH program and the BASIC program. See Section II for more details.

Example

To use the font selection program for the Z cartridge, copy all the files from the CART-Z directory of the distribution diskette to your current directory with the command:

```
COPY A:\CART-Z\*.* [name of target directory]
```

To display the menu of choices, start the FONT-Z.BAT program by typing:

```
FONT-Z
```

The menu for the Z cartridge will be displayed on the screen and should correspond to Figure 1.1 below.

```
             Hewlett Packard LaserJet Font Menu
                       Cartridge Z-1a

               1. Helvetica 8 Medium Portrait
               2. Helvetica 10 Medium Portrait
               3. Helvetica 10 Bold Portrait
               4. Helvetica 10 Italic Portrait
               5. Helvetica 12 Medium Portrait
               6. Helvetica 12 Bold Portrait
               7. Helvetica 12 Italic Portrait
               8. Helvetica 14 Bold Portrait

               9. Times Roman 8 Medium Portrait
              10. Times Roman 10 Medium Portrait
              11. Times Roman 10 Bold Portrait
              12. Times Roman 10 Italic Portrait
              13. Times Roman 12 Medium Portrait
              14. Times Roman 12 Bold Portrait
              15. Times Roman 12 Italic Portrait
              16. Times Roman 14 Bold Portrait

              17. Line Printer 8 Medium Portrait
-------------------------------------------------------
                       Enter Selection
```

Figure 1.1 Z-CART font menu.

To make a selection such as Times Roman 12 Point Bold Portrait, enter the selection number, **14**, at the prompt and press

<RETURN>. The program will execute and return you to the DOS prompt. To exit from the menu without selecting a font change, enter **0**, or press **<RETURN>** without entering a value. If you should press **<ESC>**, the prompt will be erased. Press **<RETURN>** to resume.

Notes

1. You must have both the .BAT and .BAS files loaded in the same directory for these programs to operate together.
   To create new sets of BASIC and BATCH files for another font cartridge, it is easiest to copy one of the existing sets and alter the names and contents to fit the new cartridge. You can use the BASIC editor supplied with BASIC to modify the selection codes in the BASIC programs, and the EDLIN editor supplied with DOS to modify the BATCH programs.
2. The BASIC programs and their associated BATCH files, including the menu listing program FONT-[X].BAS (where X = the cartridge letter for HP cartridges) are isolated in individual directories corresponding to the font cartridge they support. This facilitates copying only those files required for your particular need. (Note that the JetWare JetFont 123 programs are located in a directory Lotica.)
3. BASIC and BATCH files are included on the Laser-ToolKit Utility diskette for the most popular font cartridges. You can create similar program systems for other cartridges by copying the structure of one of the samples and inserting the names and codes appropriate for your selected cartridge.
4. If BASIC isn't available on your system, because you use an accelerator or other enhancement board, you may have to shift to BASICA or some other version of the BASIC interpreter. Contact your board manufacturer for information. If you do use another named version of the BASIC interpreter, you will have to modify the batch files, substituting the new version of the interpreter for BASIC (e.g., substitute BASICA for BASIC, and make sure that BASICA.COM is available on your system).

dBASE III PLUS PROGRAMS

COMPRESS.PRG

Directory Location: Root

Software Required: dBASE III

Application: Changes font to Line Printer Medium Portrait.

Description and Usage

This is a stand-alone utility subroutine that can be called from within any other dBASE program file or run directly from the dot prompt. To switch a report into Line Printer type font, you must execute this subroutine before calling the report. This is accomplished with the command:

```
DO COMPRESS
```

You must also change the report width and length parameters to 132 columns by 60 lines for letter-sized paper or 132 columns by 89 lines for legal-sized paper with the command:

```
MODIFY REPORT Reportname
```

To return your printer to the normal Courier 10 type font after the report, follow the report with the command:

```
DO NORMAL
```

Example

If you wanted to print the report named SALES in Line Printer Portrait type font on letter-sized paper, first modify the report to set the width to 132 columns and the length to 60 lines with the command:

```
MODIFY REPORT SALES
```

Then enter the following commands in your program file:

```
DO COMPRESS
REPORT FORM SALES
DO NORMAL
```

Caution

You must run the COMPRESS program before calling the report. You must also set the width and length of the report prior to calling it.

LANDCOMP.PRG

Directory Location: Root

Software Required: dBASE III

Application: Changes font to Line Printer Medium Landscape.

Description and Usage

This is a stand-alone utility subroutine that can be called from within any other dBASE program file or run directly from the dot prompt. To switch a report into Line Printer Landscape type font, you must execute this subroutine before calling the report. This is accomplished with the command:

```
DO LANDCOMP
```

You must also change the report width and length parameters to 176 columns by 60 lines for letter-sized paper or 226 columns by 60 lines for legal paper with the command:

```
MODIFY REPORT Reportname
```

To return your printer to the normal Courier 10 Portrait type font after the report, follow the report with the command:

```
DO NORMAL
```

Example

If you want to print the report named SALES in Line Printer Landscape type font on letter-sized paper, first modify the report to set the width to 176 columns and the length to 60 lines with the command:

```
MODIFY REPORT SALES
```

Then enter the following commands in your program file:

```
DO LANDCOMP
REPORT FORM SALES
DO NORMAL
```

Caution

You must run the LANDCOMP program before calling the report. You must also set the width and length of the report prior to calling it.

LANDNORM.PRG

Directory Location: Root

Software Required: dBASE III

Application: Changes font to Courier 10 Landscape.

Description and Usage

This is a stand-alone utility subroutine that can be called from within any other program file or run directly from the dot prompt. To switch a report into Courier 10 Landscape type font, you must execute this subroutine before calling the report. This is accomplished with the command:

```
DO LANDNORM
```

You must also change the report width and length parameters to 106 columns by 45 lines for letter-sized paper or 136 columns by 45 lines for legal paper with the command:

```
MODIFY REPORT Reportname
```

To return your printer to the normal Courier 10 Portrait type font after the report, follow the report with the command:

```
DO NORMAL
```

Example

If you want to print the report named SALES in Courier 10 Landscape type font on letter-sized paper, first modify the report to set the width to 106 columns and the length to 45 lines with the command:

```
MODIFY REPORT SALES
```

Then enter the following commands in your program file:

```
DO LANDNORM
REPORT FORM SALES
DO NORMAL
```

Caution

You must run the LANDCOMP program before calling the report. You must set the width and length of the report prior to calling it.

LOTICA LT??-???.PRG

Directory Location: Root

Software Required: dBASE III Plus

Application: Changes font to one of the Lotica compressed fonts.

Description and Usage

These are stand-alone utility subroutines that can be called from within any other dBASE program file or run directly from the dot prompt. The question marks in the program names refer to the 14 different fonts and programs available. The first number refers to the pitch size, and the second represents the lines per inch. The final letter stands for Landscape or Portrait orientation.

LT12-8P thus means 12 pitch type with eight lines per inch in Portrait orientation. To switch a report into one of the Lotica compressed fonts, you must execute this subroutine before calling the report. You must also change the report width and length parameters according to Table 1.1.

To switch to, say, Lotica 30 pitch, 16 lines per-inch Portrait font for letter-sized paper, use the command:

```
DO LT30-16P
```

and set the report width to 230 columns and the length to 160 lines. In the same fashion, to select the Lotica 16 pitch, eight lines per-inch Landscape font for legal paper, use the command:

```
DO LT16-8L
```

And set the report width to 208 and the length to 60 lines with the command:

```
MODIFY REPORT Reportname
```

Place First Class
Postage Here
Post Office
Will Not Deliver
Without Postage

Brady Books
15 Columbus Circle
New York, NY 10023

ATT: J. Padlad

Table 1.1 Lotica width tables

JetWare - JetFont 123 Cartridge
Lotica Fonts
Width Table for dBASE III

PORTRAIT

Font	LETTER Length	LETTER Width	LEGAL Length	LEGAL Width
LT12-6P	60	90	78	90
LT12-8P	80	90	104	90
LT16-8P	80	120	104	120
LT16-12P	120	120	156	120
LT21-12P	120	160	156	160
LT21-16P	160	160	208	160
LT30-16P	160	230	208	230

LANDSCAPE

Font	LETTER Length	LETTER Width	LEGAL Length	LEGAL Width
LT12-6L	45	120	45	156
LT12-8L	60	120	60	156
LT16-8L	60	160	60	208
LT16-12L	90	160	90	208
LT21-12L	90	210	90	273
LT21-16L	120	210	120	273
LT30-16L	120	300	120	390

To return your printer to the normal Courier 10 type font after the report, follow the report with the command:

```
DO NORMAL
```

Example

If you want to print the report named SALES in Lotica 30 pitch landscape on legal paper, first modify the report to set the width to 390 columns and the length to 120 lines with the command:

```
MODIFY REPORT SALES
```

Then enter the following commands in your program file:

```
DO LT30-16L
REPORT FORM SALES
DO NORMAL
```

Caution

You must run the LT??-??? program before calling the report. You must also set the width and length of the report prior to calling it.

NORMAL.PRG

Directory Location: Root

Software Required: dBASE III Plus

Application: Changes font to Courier 10 Medium Portrait.

Description and Usage

This is a stand-alone utility subroutine that can be called from within any other dBASE program file or run directly from the dot prompt. To switch a report into Courier 10 Portrait type font, you must execute this subroutine before calling the report. This is accomplished with the command:

```
DO NORMAL
```

You must also change the report width and length parameters to 80 columns by 60 lines for letter-sized paper or 80 columns by 89 lines for legal paper with the command:

```
MODIFY REPORT Reportname
```

Example

If you want to print the report named SALES in Courier 10 Portrait type font on letter-sized paper, first modify the report to set the width to 80 columns and the length to 60 lines with the command:

```
MODIFY REPORT SALES
```

Then enter the following commands in your program file:

```
DO NORMAL
REPORT FORM SALES
```

Caution

You must run the NORMAL program before calling the report. You must also set the width and length of the report prior to calling it.

RESET.PRG

Directory Location: Root

Software Required: dBASE III Plus

Application: Resets the printer to the User Default Environment.

Usage

This is a stand-alone utility subroutine that can be called from within any other dBASE program file or run directly from the dot prompt. To reset the printer to the User Default Environment at any time, you need only run this command:

```
DO RESET
```

This is especially useful at the beginning of a program or as part of the report printing routines. Since the **RESET** command clears the printer of any data stored in the print buffer but not yet printed, you may want to issue an **EJECT** command prior to the **RESET**.

Example

To reset the printer from the dot prompt, enter the following command from the prompt:

```
. DO RESET
```

Caution

The **RESET** command will abandon any data left in the print buffer but not yet printed. You may want to issue an **EJECT** command prior to the **RESET** command. Placing the **EJECT** command in a program file may, however, cause you to eject many blank pages, so it should be used with discretion.

LOTUS 1-2-3
MACROS

123-MACRO P_HP_GLOBAL

Directory Location: Root

Software Required: Lotus 1-2-3 Release 2 or 2.01

Application: Used to set the margins, printer interface and the setup string for 1-2-3 worksheets to take advantage of compressed and landscape fonts.

General Macro Installation

All the 1-2-3 macros reside in a worksheet named 123-MACRO.WK1. You must copy the specific macro you wish to use to your worksheet prior to using it. This is done using the **/File Com**bine **C**opy **N**amed range command and then supplying the range name (e.g., P_HP_GLOBAL) that has been assigned to this macro. For a complete index of the macro names in the 123-MACRO.WK1, refer to the top-left corner of the worksheet or to Table 1.2 (see page 26). Each macro is seven columns wide and about 50 lines long, so be sure that you have enough room in your current worksheet to accommodate it.

Once you have copied the macro to your current worksheet, you must name the ranges that it contains. This is easier than it initially sounds, since all the range names except one are already contained in the leftmost column of each macro. You need only add the \name that you wish to assign to the macro in your worksheet. Remember that with 1-2-3, you must give each macro a two-character name consisting of the \(backslash) character and a single letter from A–Z. This name is inserted as a label with a label prefix in the top-left corner of the macro underneath the first row of asterisks. Simply place the cell pointer on this cell and enter the name with a label prefix (e.g., '\Z) and press **<RETURN>**. The name will appear in the cell.

The next step is to use the column of range names to name their associated ranges. This is done by placing the cell pointer on the top name (it should already be there) and entering the command:

```
/ Range Name Labels Right
```

This will leave you in point mode. Press the **<END>** followed by the **<DOWN>** arrow key. This will highlight the entire left column of the macro containing all the range names.

Finally, press the **<RETURN>** key and all the ranges will be properly named. You can now start the macro by pressing the **<ALT>** key and the letter name you assigned to the macro above (e.g., **<ALT><Z>**). That's all there is to it.

Description and Usage

The P_HP_GLOBAL macro inserts the specified setup string into the current worksheet, using the /**P**rint **P**rinter **O**ptions **S**etup command. You can select from among the eight options listed on a menu of choices. In addition, the macro changes the left, right, top, and bottom margins and the page length to their optimal values.

The macro also sets the interface to Serial Port # 1 using 9600 Baud. If you are using another interface such as LPT1: with a LaserJet Plus or LaserJet Series II, you will have to change line 4 of the macro accordingly (e.g., for LPT1:, line 4 would be I1).

Executing the Macro

To start the macro, press the macro starting key combination **<ALT><X>** where **X** represents the key you assigned during installation. You will be presented with a menu of font, spacing, and orientation choices. Make your selection by entering the corresponding number and pressing **<RETURN>**. You can start the macro from anywhere in your worksheet; it will return there after it has finished.

Example

To select Line Printer Landscape with 66 lines per page, start the macro and select option #8 from the menu. It's that easy.

Caution

As with any Lotus 1-2-3 macro, be careful when adding or deleting rows or columns in the worksheet to avoid interfering with the macro.

Table 1.2 Lotus 1-2-3 macro names

P_MACRO Index	
P_HP_GLOBAL	H.P. Laser Printer Global Format Setting- Generic
P_HP_B_INLINE	H.P. Laser Printer In-Line Printer Control - Cartridge B
P_HP_C_INLINE	H.P. Laser Printer In-Line Printer Control - Cartridge C
P_HP_E_INLINE	H.P. Laser Printer In-Line Printer Control - Cartridge E
P_HP_F_INLINE	H.P. Laser Printer In-Line Printer Control - Cartridge F
P_HP_G_INLINE	H.P. Laser Printer In-Line Printer Control - Cartridge G
P_HP_H_INLINE	H.P. Laser Printer In-Line Printer Control - Cartridge H
P_HP_L_INLINE	H.P. Laser Printer In-Line Printer Control - Cartridge L
P_HP_U_INLINE	H.P. Laser Printer In-Line Printer Control - Cartridge U
P_HP_X_INLINE	H.P. Laser Printer In-Line Printer Control - Cartridge X
P_HP_Y_INLINE	H.P. Laser Printer In-Line Printer Control - Cartridge Y
P_HP_Z_INLINE	H.P. Laser Printer In-Line Printer Control - Cartridge Z
P_LT123_GLOBAL	H.P. Laser Printer Global Format Setting - Lotica 123 Cartridge
P_LT123_INLINE	H.P. Laser Printer In-Line Printer Control - Lotica 123 Cartridge

123-MACRO P_HP_?_INLINE

? = A,B,C,G,H,J,L,M,N,R,T,Y,Z corresponding to each cartridge

Directory Location: Root

Software Required: Lotus 1-2-3 Release 2 or 2.01

Application: Used to insert embedded inline print commands into the body of a worksheet in order to change the font of a headline or title.

General Macro Installation

See the installation section in P_HP_GLOBAL for detailed instructions for loading and naming 1-2-3 macros. Each font cartridge has its own macro stored in 123MACRO.WK1. Their names correspond to the title of this section with the appropriate cartridge identifier substituted for the ? mark; for example, the macro name for the *Z* cartridge is P_HP_Z_INLINE. Copy the desired macro to your current worksheet, name it, and assign the range names as described in P_HP_GLOBAL.

Description and Usage

The P_HP_?_INLINE macro inserts the specified setup string into the current worksheet by inserting a new line at the current cursor location and copying the selected printer command string to the new cell immediately above the current cell. This new line will contain only the printer command and will not be printed. It is critical that the inline printer command be placed in the leftmost column of the print range. If it is not positioned there the printer command will not work. It is your responsibility to place the cursor in the leftmost column of the print range prior to initiating this macro.

Executing the Macro

After positioning the cursor, you can start the macro and make your font selection from the menu. Be sure to reset your font to the body type after your headline or title. Most of the LaserJet's headline fonts are proportional fonts. 1-2-3 does not support proportional fonts; it does not perform the spacing calculations necessary to properly align columns of text. For this reason, proportional fonts are not recommended for the body text of worksheets, but they can be used effectively for titles and headlines (see Figures 1.2 (a) and (b)).

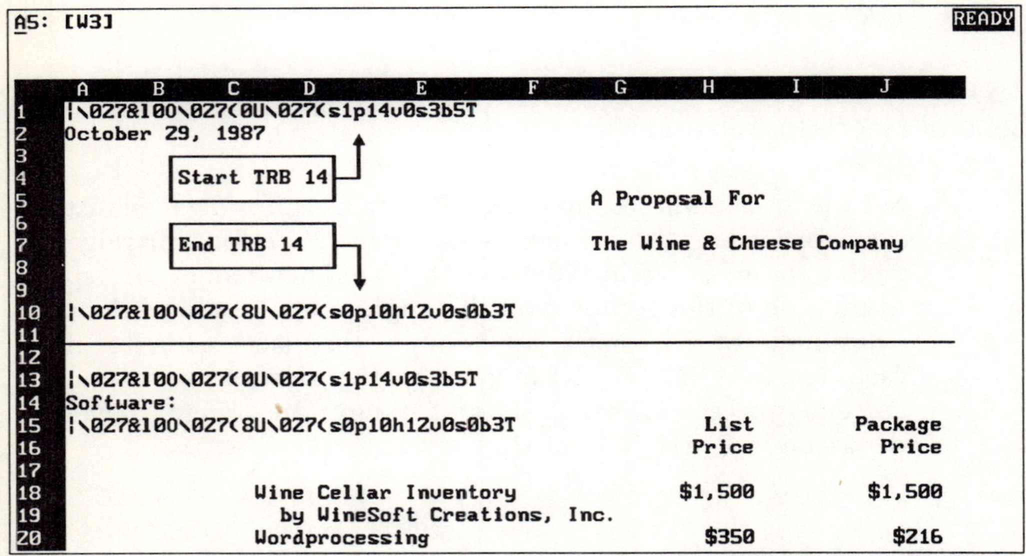

Figure 1.2(a) Inserting column heading codes in a Lotus 1-2-3 worksheet.

Example

To select Times Roman 14 for a headline as shown in Figures 1.2 (a) and (b), select the P_HP_Z_INLINE macro from the 123MACRO.WK1 worksheet. After copying and naming the macro, place the cursor in the leftmost cell of the first line you wish to alter.

October 29, 1987

A Proposal For

The Wine & Cheese Company

Software:

		Price	Price
	Wine Cellar Inventory by WineSoft Creations, Inc.	$1,500	$1,500
	Wordprocessing	$350	$216
	Telecommunications	$145	$119
Hardware:			
	XMD Model 775 w/ Color Monitor 640 k & 20 Meg HD	$2,890	$2,284
	TeleSciences 1200 Baud Modem	$350	$216
	Helios Laser Printer	$2,595	$1,800
Total:		---------	---------
		$7,830	$6,135

Figure 1.2(b) Results of inserting font codes in a worksheet.

Start the macro and select the Times Roman 14 point font from the menu. The appropriate printer command will be inserted in a new line above the desired headline. Be sure to place a printer command that selects an appropriate body text font under the title or headline, and be sure to install the selected font cartridge in your printer before attempting to print.

Cautions

Do not attempt to change the orientation of the print on a single page. The orientation change will cause the first part of the page to be printed; the page will be ejected before the next part is printed in the new orientation.

As with any Lotus 1-2-3 macro, be careful when adding or deleting rows or columns in the worksheet to avoid interfering with the macro.

Note: The inline print macros contain a page eject command that can be inserted to control the pagination of a long worksheet.

123-MACRO P_LT123_GLOBAL
(for use with JetWare JetFont 123 Cartridge)

Directory Location: Root

Software Required: Lotus 1-2-3 Release 2 or 2.01

Application: Used to set the margins, printed interface, and the setup string for 1-2-3 worksheets to take advantage of JetFont Lotica compressed and landscape fonts.

General Macro Installation

See the installation section in P_HP_GLOBAL for detailed instructions for loading and naming 1-2-3 macros. The JetFont 123 cartridge has its own macro stored in 123MACRO.WK1 called P_LT123_GLOBAL. Copy the macro to your current worksheet, name it, and assign the range names as described in P_HP_GLOBAL.

Description and Usage

The P_LT123_GLOBAL macro inserts the specified setup string into the current worksheet, using the /**P**rint **P**rinter **O**ptions **S**etup command. You can select from among the 14 options listed on a menu of choices. In addition, the macro changes the left, right, top, and bottom margins and the page length to their optimal values. See Table 1.3 for the maximum column and page length setting for the Lotica 1-2-3 fonts.

Table 1.3 Lotica font guide

JetWare - JetFont 123 Cartridge
Lotica Fonts
Width Table for Lotus 1-2-3

PORTRAIT

Font	LETTER Length	LETTER Width	LEGAL Length	LEGAL Width
LT12-6P	60	90	78	90
LT12-8P	80	90	100	90
LT16-8P	80	120	100	120
LT16-12P	100	120	100	120
LT21-12P	100	160	100	160
LT21-16P	100	160	100	160
LT30-16P	100	230	100	230

LANDSCAPE

Font	LETTER Length	LETTER Width	LEGAL Length	LEGAL Width
LT12-6L	45	120	45	156
LT12-8L	60	120	60	156
LT16-8L	60	160	60	208
LT16-12L	90	160	90	208
LT21-12L	90	210	90	240
LT21-16L	100	210	100	240
LT30-16L	100	240	100	240

The macro sets the interface to Serial Port 1 using 9600 Baud. If you are using another interface such as LPT1: with a LaserJet PLUS or LaserJet Series II, you will have to change line 4 of the macro accordingly (e.g., for LPT1:, line 4 would be I1).

Executing the Macro

To start the macro, press the macro starting key combination **<ALT> <X>** where **X** represents the key you assigned during installation. You will be presented with a menu of font, spacing, and orientation choices. Make your selection by entering the corresponding number and pressing **<RETURN>**. You can start the macro from anywhere in your worksheet; it will return there after it has finished.

Example

To select Lotica 30 pitch with 16 lines per inch in Landscape orientation, start the macro and select option #17 from the menu. It's that easy.

Caution

As with any Lotus 1-2-3 macro, be careful when adding or deleting rows or columns in the worksheet to avoid interfering with the macro.

123-MACRO P_LT123_INLINE
(for use with JetWare JetFont 123 Cartridge)

Directory Location: Root

Software Required: Lotus 1-2-3 Release 2 or 2.01

Application: Used to insert embedded inline print commands into the body of a worksheet in order to change the font of a headline or title.

General Macro Installation

See the installation section in P_HP_GLOBAL for detailed instructions for loading and naming 1-2-3 macros. The JetFont 123 Cartridge has its own macro stored in 123MACRO.WK1 called P_LT123_INLINE. Copy the macro to your current worksheet, name it, and assign the range names as described in P_HP_GLOBAL.

Description and Usage

The P_LT123_INLINE macro inserts the specified setup string into the current worksheet by inserting a new line at the current cursor location and copying the selected printer command string to the new cell immediately above the current cell. This new line will contain only the printer command and will not be printed. It is critical that the inline printer command be placed in the leftmost column of the print range. If it is not located there the printer command will not work. It is your responsibility to place the cursor in the leftmost column of the print range prior to initiating this macro.

Executing the Macro

After positioning the cursor, you can start the macro and make your font selection from the menu. Be sure to reset your font to the body type after your headline or title.

All the Lotica fonts are fixed-pitch fonts, making them perfect for Lotus 1-2-3, which does not support proportional fonts. The extremely small point size of the font allows you to place the full 240 characters on a line. This is actually a limit of 1-2-3. The Lotica 30 pitch font in landscape orientation could print 390 characters a line on legal paper.

The inline print commands do not change the page margins or lines per page. You will have to experiment with various settings to accommodate the combination of font sizes that you actually use on a given page.

Example

To select Lotica 21 pitch 16 LPI for a calculation detail, select the P_LT123_INLINE macro from the 123MACRO.WK1 worksheet. After copying and naming the macro, place the cursor in the left-most cell of the first line that you wish to alter. Start the macro and select the Lotica 21-16 font from the menu. The appropriate printer command will be inserted in a new line above the desired section. Be sure to place a printer command that selects an appropriate full body font under the detail, and be sure to install the JetFont 123 cartridge in your printer before attempting to print.

Caution

Do not attempt to change the orientation of the print on a single page. The orientation change will cause the first part of the page to be printed, and the page will be ejected before the next part of the page is printed in the new orientation.

As with any Lotus 1-2-3 macro, be careful when adding or deleting rows or columns in the worksheet to avoid interfering with the macro.

Note

The inline print macros contain a page eject command that can be inserted to control the pagination of a long worksheet.

WORDPERFECT MACROS

COLLATE.MAC & COLLATE1.MAC
(for use with Version 4.2)
COLLATE.WPM & COLLATE1.WPM
(for use with Version 5.0)

Directory Location: Root

Software Required: WordPerfect 4.2 or 5.0

Application: Reverses the page print order so that material printed on face-down collating printers such as the Classic LaserJet and LaserJet PLUS will be properly collated.

Principle

The macro operates by moving to the last page of the document and printing it as a single page. It then moves up one page and prints that. This process is repeated until the entire document is printed. The initial placement is performed by COLLATE.MAC, and the repeated printing is performed by COLLATE1.MAC. You must copy both macros for the process to work. The macros with the .WPM extension are for use with WordPerfect 5.0.

Description and Usage

The macros can be started anywhere in the current document and will print the entire document. The macros must be placed either in the current directory or the WordPerfect directory for Version 4.2. With Version 5.0 you also have the option of placing your macros in a dedicated macro directory. You can either maintain the current names or rename the COLLATE macro to an **<ALT>** key macro name to facilitate starting. Do not rename the COLLATE1 macro.

Example

If you maintain the current macro name, start the macro by pressing **<ALT><F10>** and entering the macro name COLLATE. After you press **<RETURN>**, the document will print in reverse page order. If you rename the COLLATE macro to ALTC.MAC, you can start the macro by pressing and holding the **<ALT>** key while you press the **<C>** key.

Caution

Do not rename COLLATE1.MAC (4.2) or COLLATE1.WPM (5.0). They call themselves as part of their operation and must retain their assigned names. You can rename the starting macros COLLATE.MAC (4.2) and COLLATE.WPM (5.0).

ENVELOP1.MAC & ENVELOP2.MAC
(for use with Version 4.2)
ENVELOP1.WPM & ENVELOP2.WPM
(for use with Version 5.0)

Directory Location: Root

Software Required: WordPerfect 4.2 or 5.0

Application: Prints the address from the top of a memo on an envelope. ENVELOP1 is for use with the LaserJet and LaserJet PLUS, while ENVELOP2 is for use with the LaserJet Series II.

Principle

Captures the address at the top of a memo, moves it to a new page, and then prints the page, pausing for the user to supply a suitable font for landscape printing on an envelope. Finally, it deletes the new page and returns to the top of the memo.

Description and Usage

The macros must be placed either in the current directory or the WordPerfect directory for Version 4.2. With Version 5.0 you also have the option of placing your macros in a dedicated macro directory. You can either maintain the current names or rename the ENVELOP1 or ENVELOP2 macro to an **<ALT>** key macro name to facilitate starting.

Place the cursor at the beginning of the address, then invoke the macro. At the first pause, enter the pitch of the desired font. At the second pause, enter the number of the desired font. You must select a landscape font. The address will print immediately so it's best to place an envelope in the manual feed position before starting the macro.

Example

If you are using a LaserJet Series II, place an envelope in the centered manual feed slot before you start the macro. If you maintain the current macro name, place the cursor on the first letter of the address and start the macro by pressing **<ALT> <F10>** and entering the macro name ENVELOP1 or ENVELOP2. If you are using a Series II and want to use Courier 10 Landscape, enter **10** (pitch) at the first pause and **3** (font #) at the second pause. The address will be printed on the envelope.

Caution

The macro searches for the two hard returns that follow the address, forming one or more blank lines under the address. The address itself must not contain a blank line, and there must be at least one blank line following the address.

Note

ENVELOP1 formats the envelope for use with printers such as an HP LaserJet or LaserJet PLUS that feature left-aligned manual paper feed. Use ENVELOP2 with center manual feed printers such as the HP LaserJet Series II.

The 5.0 versions of the macros assume that you have properly installed a printer with a resident or cartridge-based landscape font. It does not pause for you to provide the font specification, but rather defaults to the Landscape font closest to the font used for the text of the memo.

FONT.MAC, FONT1.MAC & FONT2.MAC
(for use with Version 4.2)

Directory Location: Root

Software Required: WordPerfect 4.2 only

Application: Use to easily change the font of a block of text and return to the previous font after the defined block

Principle

The macro pauses to allow you to highlight the text block that you wish to change. It then pauses to allow you to enter the new font specifications. Next, it searches backward for the previous font definition code. If it finds one, it invokes the submacro FONT1, which copies the code and inserts it at the end of the text block. If it fails to find one, it invokes the submacro FONT2, which inserts the default code

```
[Font Change:10,1]
```

at the end of the text block. In this way it places the new font specification in front of the block and the previous font specification after the block.

Usage

Place the cursor on the first character of the block you wish to change. At the first pause, highlight the entire block to be changed and press <**RETURN**>. At the second pause, enter the specifications of the new font (Pitch and Font Number). The macro will place the font specification before and after the defined block.

You can either maintain the current names or rename the FONT macro to an <**ALT**> key macro name to facilitate starting. Do not rename the FONT1 or FONT2 macros.

Example

Suppose that you have renamed the primary macro FONT.MAC to ALTF.MAC to facilitate starting and are using Courier 10 as the default font of a memo. After typing the memo, you have decided that you want to highlight a quote in the memo by changing it to italics. This requires a font change in WordPerfect 4.2. Place the cursor on the first letter of the quote and start the macro by pressing **<ALT>** **<F>**. At the first pause, you use the cursor keys to highlight the entire quote and press **<RETURN>**. At the second pause, enter **10** for the pitch and **3** for the font number. (Appropriate numbers for a LaserJet Series II, these may vary depending on the fonts available on your printer.) The macro will then place the font changes before and after the quote.

Caution

Do not rename FONT1.MAC or FONT2.MAC. They are called FONT.MAC as part of their operation and must retain their assigned names. You can rename the starting macro FONT.MAC to a short starting name if you wish.

II A PCL PRIMER

Highlights

- Who Should Learn the PCL Printer Language?
- Components of a PCL Command.
- PCL Printer Language Grammar.
- The Structure of PCL Printer Language Commands.
- Creating PCL Printer Language Commands: Single Commands.
- Commands with Variables—"Parameterized Commands."
- Combining Commands.
- The PCL Page.
- Logical Page, Physical Page, Printable Area, Text Area.
- Sending PCL Printer Language Commands to the Printer.
- Batch Files and BASIC.
- Issuing PCL Printer Language Commands from Application Software.
- dBASE III Plus.
- Lotus 1-2-3.
- Word Perfect.
- Other Application Programs.
- Raster Graphics.
- Rectangular Fill Graphics.
- Soft Font Creation.
- Macros.
- Defining a Macro.
- Deleting a Macro.
- Patience Is the PCL Programmer's Greatest Asset.

Printer Speak

Every printer must respond to a set of codes from the computer to put characters in the right place, set margins, set the pitch, and so on. LaserJet printers are no exception; to create a page, the computer must instruct the printer about what to do with each dot. With the LaserJets, the codes comprise more than a simple laundry list of numbers; rather, they are used in a programming language called

Printer Command Language (PCL), which HP wrote specifically for the LaserJet family.

A programming language, like a natural language, has grammatical rules and a vocabulary. The rules determine which "sentences" are valid, and the vocabulary conveys the meaning of the sentences. The grammar of the PCL printer language is also *generative*; that is, from a small set of rules, you can generate many valid sentences, each of which instructs the printer to perform a different function, such as selecting fonts or altering the number of lines per page. By understanding the basic grammatical rules, you can combine "words" (i.e., command codes) from PCL's vocabulary and instruct your printer to carry out any desired action.

Who Should Learn the PCL Printer Language?

Many software programs support the LaserJet printers. Once you install them, they know which PCL printer language commands to issue to carry out various actions. The knowledge about your LaserJet (or any printer) is contained in a special file called a *Printer Driver*. Drivers for LaserJet printers contain PCL codes; drivers for Epson printers contain the command codes designed for Epsons. If a software program has drivers for a LaserJet printer, once you've gone through the program's installation routine you can print the most sophisticated page without ever entering a single PCL printer language command code yourself.

Why bother to learn a new language if the software takes care of it for you? If you only plan on using software that has LaserJet printer drivers, or if you never plan on using any other font but the default Courier 10 pitch that resides in the printer, you really don't need to bother. But if you plan to use your LaserJet printer with one of the many software packages that do not explicitly support it and you wish to change fonts, shift to a bold or italic typeface, or alter the margins, you will have to do it yourself, which means you will have to learn how to read and write PCL printer language commands.

Even if you don't plan on writing your own PCL printer language commands, we advise browsing through this chapter. Any time you don't understand why a piece of hardware or software is performing an action, you are at the mercy of the equipment and will be less likely to help yourself when unusual situations arise. Without a cursory understanding of PCL, your LaserJet printer will remain a black box. This section is designed to open the lid of that box. It provides an explanation of the grammatical rules of the language, giving plenty of practical examples.

An Overview of PCL Printer Language: Grammar

A New Approach

When Hewlett-Packard introduced the Classic LaserJet printer, it had to decide whether to copy one of the existing printer languages, either the one used for Diablo printers (long regarded as the standard for thimble or daisy-wheel printers) or the one designed for IBM/Epson printers (the standard for dot-matrix printers). Unfortunately, neither the Diablo nor the IBM/Epson languages was adequate for the complex task of controlling a 300 dot per inch page printer, so HP started from scratch and created the PCL printer language, which is uniquely suited to the demands of its LaserJet printers.

While PCL differs from other printer command languages in structure and complexity, it nevertheless shares many features of its predecessors. For example, PCL printer language instructions are sometimes called *Escape Sequences* since they all start with the ASCII Escape character. ASCII is the acronym for The American Standard Code for Information Interchange, which defines the numerical codes used by computers and printers to represent the various possible letters, numbers, and special characters. The Escape character or code is the unprintable character assigned to the **<ESC>** key by some software. Since it is unprintable, it is often represented by its decimal ASCII number 027. If you have used printer commands before to control programs such as Lotus 1-2-3, you will recognize the ASCII Escape character. (For example, in 1-2-3 you enter **\027 015** through the **\P**rint **P**rinter **O**ptions **S**etup command to set an IBM/Epson dot-matrix printer into the compressed print mode.)

The Nature of the PCL Printer Language

As its name implies, Printer Command Language is indeed a type of computer programming language. Unlike most other computer languages such as BASIC, Fortran, or C, however, PCL is relatively limited and is used primarily to issue individual directive commands, such as *do this* and then *do that.* There is no provision for decision making, so the printer either understands the intent of your command and executes it immediately, or it fails to understand your intent and ignores your command altogether.

Most PCL printer language commands are also *State Change* in nature, which means that they change the current operating state or values of the printer. For example, if the printer were prepared to print a page with a one-inch left margin, one inch would be considered the current value or state for the left margin. The printer would continue to print with a one-inch left margin ad infinitum until you were to issue the correct command for another left margin value, say two inches. Two inches would then become the new current value. The printer will then continue to print two-inch margins until you change it again or issue a reset command. When you reset the printer, either by turning it off or by pressing the **RESET** button (LaserJet Series II printer), it will return to its "default configuration" with each of the key values returned to its initial state (all LaserJets have a default left margin of about one-quarter of an inch). The default configuration is set by permanent software contained in the logic of the printer, or, in the case of the LaserJet Series II, it can be set by the user from the control panel at the time of setup.

Another way to look at a PCL printer is that it uses a printer configuration or environment consisting of many different parameters (page length, left margin, font, etc.), each of which is assigned a value. Each parameter is set to its default value at the time of printer startup or reset. Each parameter will remain fixed until it is specifically set to another value by the user or the user's software.

Components of a PCL Printer Language Command

As with all programming languages, the PCL printer language has a command vocabulary and a specific grammar for its use. The combination of a vocabulary and a grammar allows the user to create

PCL printer language commands for specific purposes. More importantly, it permits the creation of new and unique complex commands from the proper combination of simple commands. While this opens the door for a virtually unlimited number of commands to be built with the PCL printer language, most people find that they repeatedly use the same group of relatively simple commands. The complex ones are more commonly used by graphics and other application software when they communicate directly with your printer.

As we mentioned above, PCL printer language commands are sometimes called *Escape Sequences* or *Escape Commands* because they all start with the Escape character Ec (ASCII value 027). This character is used to tell the printer that the characters following the Escape character represent a PCL command. The printer reads the PCL commands and, rather than trying to print them, splits them from the character and graphic data via a process called *Parsing*. Once split off from the characters and graphic elements, the PCL printer language commands are either executed immediately if they affect the entire page (e.g., a paper size command) or are executed in their proper sequence if their action should occur in the middle of a page (e.g., a font change command).

PCL Printer Language Grammar

The leading Escape character is followed by a sequence of one or more characters, including upper- and lowercase letters, numbers, and special characters such as parentheses ( ) or ampersands &. Escape sequences take the following general form:

```
Ec X y # Z data
```

where:

Ec = *Escape Character:* The introductory Escape character indicates that a printer command follows.

X = *Parameterized Character:* Indicates that the command contains variable data that the printer will have to interpret, rather than a fixed command. For example, when setting the page length, you will have to supply the number of lines on the page as a parameter. In contrast, when you issue a printer reset command, no parameter is required. The *Parameterized Character* (HP's term, not ours) alerts the printer that a parameter requiring special interpretation follows. The Parameterized Character will be one of the special ASCII characters within the range 33 through 47 (| through /). See ASCII table, Appendix D. Parameterized Characters are only used when the command requires that a parametric value be supplied with the command and interpreted by the printer. Therefore, some commands will contain a Parameterized Character while others will not.

y = Group Character: Tells the printer what type of command is being sent. This character is the primary means of distinguishing between the various types of printer commands. For example, all font selection commands contain the group selector (, while all page format commands use the group selector &, and all raster (bit-mapped) graphics commands begin with an *. The Group character is required for all PCL printer language commands. Group characters falls within the range of ASCII characters ' through ~ (decimal 39 through 126; see ASCII chart, Appendix D).

 # = Value Field: Some commands require special numerical data. These are called Parameterized Commands and are always preceded by the Parameterized Character described above. Positioning commands, for example, must indicate exactly how many spaces to move the cursor. Similarly, font selection commands require numerical data to select between various options such as symbol sets, styles, and typefaces. The Value Field may contain integers or decimal values and may be preceded by a + or – sign to indicate relative changes from the current value of the parameter (e.g., to move the cursor four lines down from the current line you would use +4 in the Value Field of the command).

Z = Terminating Character: An upper- or lowercase ASCII letter corresponding to the parameter to which the preceding value field applies. If the character is lowercase, it indicates that the command continues. If it is uppercase, it concludes the Escape sequence.

data = Certain commands are used to precede data to which they apply. For example, graphics data are preceded by a command indicating how much data follow. The number of data bytes would be defined by the value in the value field.

> **Note:** When reading or writing PCL printer language commands, it is very important to distinguish between several very similar characters, as well as upper- or lowercase representations of alphabetic characters. One of the most common group characters is the lowercase "L," "l". This must be carefully differentiated from the number 1 that is also very common in PCL printer language commands. The footnote running on the bottom of each page reiterates these characters. Likewise, you must differentiate between the uppercase letter O and zero, 0. Also, as mentioned above, PCL printer language uses the case of the terminating character of a command to indicate whether the command is finished (uppercase) or continues (lowercase).

The Structure of PCL Printer Language Commands

Three key concepts underlie the PCL printer language. First, a command starts off with the Escape character [E]c to announce that it *is* a command. Second, the command must immediately tell the printer which instruction it represents. This is communicated in the one or two characters (parameterized and group characters) following the Escape character. Note that the range of characters assigned to parameterized characters and group characters overlaps in the range ASCII numbers 39 through 47. This means that some characters can individually be used to represent a command from a parameterized group while others will require two characters to convey this information.

For example, the command used to select the Roman-8 symbol set is

```
Ec(8U
```

where the "(" character is used both as the group indicator (font selection) and as an indicator that the command is parameterized (i.e., the value 8 is assigned to the parameter U.) In contrast, to set the page length, use the command

```
Ec&l60P
```

where the letter l (lowercase "L") indicates that it is a page formatting command, but does not by itself indicate that the command will be parameterized. It is therefore preceded by the & character to indicate that it will be a parameterized page command. The value 60 is assigned to the parameter P for 60 lines per page in normal portrait orientation.

The third key concept is that the parameters for a particular variable precede the variable to which it is assigned. This is particularly important to understand before we start combining commands into more complex combined commands later in this section. Notice, for example, how the value 60 precedes the parameter P in the above example.

Creating PCL Printer Language Commands

Single Commands

Now that we've covered the components and structure of PCL printer language commands, let's look at several examples of the language in action. The first example is the simplest and the most important:

```
EcE
```

In PCL commands, the number one = 1; the lowercase letter "el" = l; the number zero = 0; and the uppercase letter "oh" = O.

This is the PCL printer reset command. It causes the printer to return to its start-up defaults for all variables. In general, it is a good idea to precede any series of PCL printer language commands with a printer reset to ensure that the commands that follow will be acting in the intended environment. This is important, since most printer commands remain in effect until they are specifically changed to something else.

For example, if the printer is set for Landscape orientation and you try to issue a font selection command for a portrait-based font without first switching to Portrait orientation, the printer will continue to remain in Landscape. When the ᴱcE command precedes your selection, all variables are reset to known default values and you can be sure that your commands will be executed as expected. (With any LaserJet you can reset the defaults by turning the printer off and then on again. With the LaserJet PLUS, 500 PLUS, and Series II printers, you can restore the printer to its defaults by pressing and holding the **CONTINUE/RESET** button for seven seconds and then releasing it.)

If your setup requires more than one command, DO NOT reset the printer before EACH command, since this will undo the effect of prior commands that you have intentionally issued. Instead, reset the printer only once before the entire series of commands.

Commands with Variables—Parameterized Commands

Many commands require that you supply variable information for one or more parameters. For example, when setting the page length or margins, you must specify the number of rows or columns to use. The number specified is called a parameter or parametric value, and commands that use them are called *parameterized commands.*

Let's say, for example, that you want to change the left margin to one inch. The command involves setting a parameter, the left margin, and therefore uses a parameterized character as part of the command. The command structure is

```
ᴱc&a#L
```

In PCL commands, the number one = 1; the lowercase letter "el" = l; the number zero = Ø; and the uppercase letter "oh" = O.

where:

^{E}c is the Escape code that precedes all printer commands,

&a indicates that you want to change a page format parameter,

will be replaced by the desired setting in column numbers, and

L indicates that it is the left margin parameter we wish to change. Moreover, the uppercase L indicates the end of the command.

To set the left margin to one inch, we need to replace the # character with a value determined by the number of Characters Per Inch (CPI) of your font. If you are using a 12 CPI font, then the value for one inch is 12. If you were using a 10 CPI font, the value is 10. Say the font is 12 CPI; the command to set the left margin to one inch is:

```
Ec&a12L
```

In the same fashion, to set the top margin to three inches, issue the command:

```
Ec&l18E
```

where:

&l = Formatting command
18 = Three inches with six lines per inch
E = Top margin

And to set the vertical line spacing to eight lines per inch, the command is:

```
Ec&l8D
```

where:

In PCL commands, the number one = 1; the lowercase letter "el" = l; the number zero = 0; and the uppercase letter "oh" = O.

&l = Formatting command
8 = Eight lines per inch
D = Vertical spacing

To select a soft font that has been downloaded and assigned ID #3 (more on this later), use the command:

^{E}c(3X

where:

(= Font command
3 = Font ID #3
X = Select font by ID number

As you can see, even parameterized commands are quite straightforward, consisting of a parameterized group identifier, the parametric value, and the character representing the parameter to be set.

Combining Commands

Most of the complexity of PCL printer language commands comes from the process of combining like commands into a single long command that can appear unfathomable at first glance. For example, the command for selecting 10 point, proportional, Times Roman, bold, upright, Portrait type font with the Roman-8 symbol set from the F cartridge could be expressed:

^{E}c&lØO^{E}c(8U^{E}c(s1p1ØvØs3b5T

This monster actually consists of three separate commands that have been strung together, each starting with the Escape character. They are generally combined because all three are required to ensure that the desired font is actually selected. These could just as easily be shown and entered separately as follows:

In PCL commands, the number one = 1; the lowercase letter "el" = l; the number zero = Ø; and the uppercase letter "oh" = O.

1. ^Ec&l0O
2. ^Ec(8U
3. ^Ec(s1p10v0s3b5T

The first command sets the paper orientation to Portrait. The parameterized group characters &l indicate that the command will be setting a format parameter. The parameter to be set is O, for orientation. In this command, the O parameter is set to the value of 0, which means Portrait orientation. The alternative is to set it to 1, which would change the orientation to landscape.

The second command selects the symbol set to be used. The single parameterized group character, (, indicates that this will be a command setting a font parameter, in this case the symbol set. The 8U combination calls for the Roman-8 symbol set. The Roman-8 symbol set is comprised of the USASCII and Roman Extension symbol sets.

The third command in the series selects the specific font. It also introduces a new concept: combining like commands from the same group into a single command. In order to save space in memory and time in transmission, and to reduce the number of key strokes required to enter a command, HP allows commands from the same group to share the same Escape and group character as parts of a continuous single command.

The rules for combining commands are straightforward:

1. They must have the exact same group character(s).
2. You must shift all terminating characters to lowercase except the very last one, which must be uppercase. The lowercase terminating characters indicate that the command continues, while the final uppercase character indicates that the command does indeed finally end.
3. You should always combine commands in the order that you want them executed from left to right.

Once again, we can break down the third command into simpler individual commands, so the command

^Ec(s1p10v0s3b5T

In PCL commands, the number one = 1; the lowercase letter "el" = l; the number zero = 0; and the uppercase letter "oh" = O.

could have been written

```
Ec(s1P  Ec(s10V  Ec(s0S  Ec(s3B  Ec(s5T
```

Note how each of the terminating characters has been shifted to uppercase to indicate that each command stands on its own and terminates before the next one begins. Also note that we would have to enter the opening code `Ec(s` five times instead of once. Here's what each component of the larger command means:

`Ec(s1P` indicates that the font will be proportional
`Ec(s10V` calls for 10 point type size
`Ec(s0S` specifies upright style
`Ec(s3B` indicates a bold stroke weight
`Ec(s5T` calls for Times Roman type face.

Recapping the meaning of the command:

```
Ec&l0O   Ec(8U   Ec(s1p10v0s3b5T
 Part1    Part2        Part 3
```

we have:

Portrait	(Part 1)
Roman-8	(Part 2)
Proportional	(Part 3)
10 Point	(Part 3)
Upright	(Part 3)
Bold	(Part 3)
Times Roman	(Part 3)

In PCL commands, the number one = 1; the lowercase letter "el" = l; the number zero = 0; and the uppercase letter "oh" = O.

which completely describes the desired font. If the font is available from one of the interchangeable font cartridges or from a downloaded soft font, the type will look like:

This is printed in Times Roman 10 point type.

until another font is selected or the printer is reset.

The PCL Page

Before you begin to create PCL printer language commands, you must understand how PCL treats a page. You have often heard the LaserJet called a page printer, because it will not begin to print a page until it has all the data it needs for the job. This allows the printer to compose the page from type and graphics commands that refer to positions all over the page in any order, while still printing the actual page one scan line at a time from top to bottom. In contrast, a daisy-wheel or dot-matrix printer must receive its printing instruction in strict printing order from the top left to the bottom right.

LaserJet printers receive the combination of PCL printer language commands and text or graphic data in the order sent and stores them in a part of memory called the *Page Intermediate*. The data are placed in their proper logical position within the Page Intermediate. The PCL printer language positions text and graphics according to their coordinates within the *Logical Page* (see below). The Logical Page can be thought of as the printer's equivalent of your computer's monitor screen. The current print location is likewise called the cursor position. The printer doesn't really have a cursor, nor can you see the logical page, but the analogy helps to visualize the positioning logic used by the PCL printer language.

Logical Page, Physical Page, Printable Area, Text Area

The best way to understand the Logical Page is to look at its relationship to the Physical Page, as shown in Figure 2.1. Due to physical limitations, LaserJet printers are unable to print all the way to the edges of the paper—the Physical Page. This creates an absolute margin of about one-sixth of an inch on the sides of the paper and one-fifth of an inch top and bottom. The area within these absolute margins is called the *Printable Area.* By setting the proper margins, you can print a character or graphic anywhere in the Printable Area. Any character that falls entirely or partially outside the Printable Area will not be printed. Graphics will terminate at the edge of the Printable Area.

The Logical Page is defined as running from the top to the bottom of the Physical Page, but contained within the left and right edges of the Printable Area. Note that the Logical Page is somewhat relative. It is limited by the Printable Area as defined by the left and right boundaries, but it nevertheless uses the top and bottom edges of the Physical Page for its top and bottom boundaries, even though the printer cannot really print all the way to the top or bottom

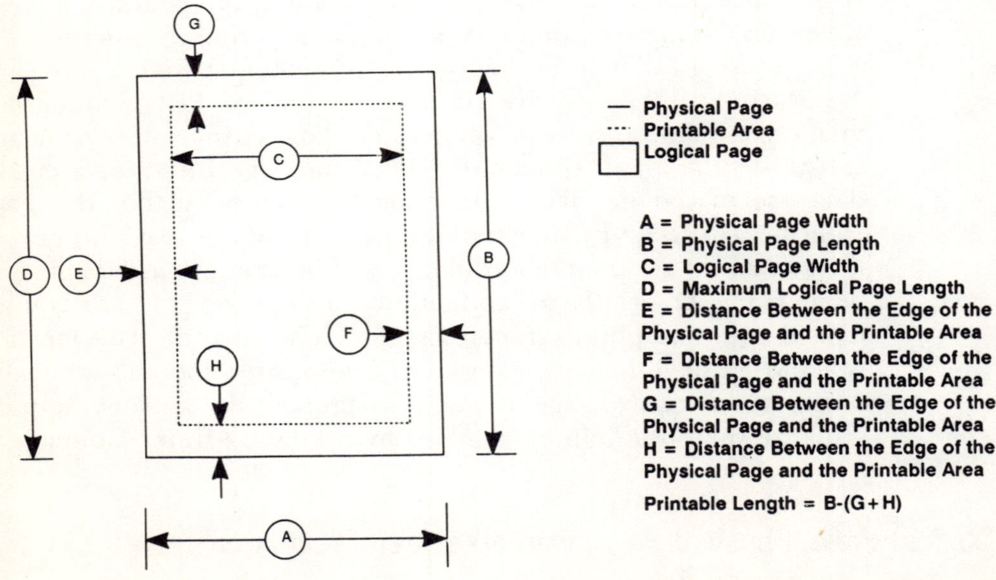

Figure 2.1 Representation of the logical page concept.

In PCL commands, the number one = 1; the lowercase letter "el" = l; the number zero = Ø; and the uppercase letter "oh" = O.

edges. Furthermore, if you change the orientation, the Logical Page also changes; it will still be limited to the area bounded by the top and bottom edges of the Physical Page and the left and right boundaries of the Printable Area, even though these boundaries now correspond to the opposite edges of the paper (long edge = top and bottom, short edge = left and right).

To further complicate matters, the top edge of the Logical Page can be moved down from the top edge of the Physical Page by setting the Top Margin. This means that the top-left corner of the Logical Page is set at the intersection of the left boundary of the Printable Area and the Position of the Top Margin. This intersection is assigned the cursor position 0,0. All other positions on the Logical Page are then referenced by their position relative to this single point. While this may seem like a complicated method for defining a starting position, it does greatly simplify all other commands because they will be relative to the upper-left corner of the Logical Page.

Now that we have established the concept of the Logical Page with the upper-left corner defined as position 0,0, we can position any character or graphic by moving the cursor to the desired position and instructing the printer to print the desired character. For example to print the character "T" at a position two inches over and three inches down from the zero point, instruct the printer to move the cursor over two inches and then down three inches. Finally, instruct the printer to print the character.

This would be simple, except that the LaserJet doesn't think in terms of inches. Instead, it uses a measurement system based on setting two key parameters: the *Horizontal Motion Index* (HMI) and the *Vertical Motion Index* (VMI). These correspond to the width of a column used for a single character in a fixed pitch type, such as Courier 10, and the height of a single line of text (really the difference between the bottoms of two adjacent lines). The HMI and VMI can be set in many different fashions and in many different units of measures. The values for the HMI and the VMI are actually stored in the printer in units of 1/3600th of an inch. You can set the value of the VMI and HMI directly by specifying them in fractions of an inch. For the VMI, the PCL printer language uses the fractional measurement of 1/48th of an inch. And for the HMI,

PCL uses 1/120th of an inch. The VMI can also be set by specifying the number of Lines Per Inch.

After setting the HMI and the VMI, you can move the cursor anywhere on the Logical Page by specifying the number of columns and rows to move. This technique is very appropriate for cursor movement with fixed pitch type. It moves the cursor in much the same fashion as that used to move the print head for a daisy-wheel or dot-matrix printer. With the LaserJet printers, however, the VMI and the HMI can vary to accommodate different sized type and can be modified to accommodate the variable pitch of proportional type.

Margins (left, right, and top), Page Length, and Text Length are set in term of the number of columns or rows that they represent. Since the physical size of a row or column varies with different settings of the HMI or VMI, the physical position of margins and page lengths set with different HMI or VMI settings varies, too.

For example, let's say we set a right margin of 60 columns with two different HMI settings. First, suppose that the HMI is set for 10 Point Prestige Elite type (12 characters per inch). This sets the HMI to 10/120, or 1/12th of an inch. This HMI is then the width of each column, so a right margin setting of 60 columns places the margin 60 × 1/12th inch or 5 inches, from the left edge of the Logical Page. A larger type, say 12 Point Courier (10 character per inch), sets the HMI to 12/120, or 1/10th of an inch. A right margin setting of 60 columns is then placed at 60 × 1/10th, or 6 inches from the left edge of the Logical Page.

This makes intuitive sense as well as mathematical sense. Sixty columns of a larger sized font should create a longer line of text than 60 columns of a smaller font. So you can see that the VMI and the HMI are very appropriate units of measure for text printing.

On the other hand, HMI and VMI are not appropriate for graphic images, since graphics are seldom drawn in such discrete fractions of an inch. PCL uses two measurement units for graphics positioning: *Dots* and *Decipoints.* Dots are the smallest printable unit and equal 1/300th of an inch. Remember that LaserJet printers can print 300 discrete dots per inch; the smallest printable unit is one such dot.

The second unit of measure, the Decipoint, corresponds to one-tenth (Deci) of a point. A *point* is the typographic unit of measure used to describe the size of type, and corresponds to 1/72nd of an inch or 1/12th of a *pica* (there are 6 picas to an inch; 1/12 × 1/6 = 1/72). A measure of 1/10th of a point therefore corresponds to 1/720th of an inch. While the LaserJet engine can't print with a resolution of 720 dots per inch (the dots and the memory requirements are too big), it can position a particular dot to the nearest 1/720th of an inch. That's all there is to positioning the cursor anywhere on the Logical Page.

Sending PCL Printer Language Commands to the Printer

Now that you've learned how to create and position a PCL printer language command, the next step in controlling the LaserJet is to transmit the command from the computer to the printer. Since the printer commands and the computer share the use of the Escape character, you can't simply press the **<ESC>** key followed by the command. The computer will react to the pressing of the **<ESC>** key in its own way depending on the operating system and software you are using.

Instead of using the **<ESC>** key, you must explicitly tell the computer to send the escape character to the printer. This is usually easily accomplished from within your software, and can always be accomplished by writing a special program in BASIC or some other programming language.

BASIC, a relatively easy to use programming language, is supplied with all PC-DOS and most MS-DOS operating systems. We will use it to demonstrate the process of transmitting commands to the printer. You can substitute any other language for BASIC as you choose. In addition, we will show how to transmit printer commands from some of the most popular application software products such as WordPerfect, dBASE III Plus, and Lotus 1-2-3.

If you are not familiar with BASIC, you should refer to the manual supplied with your computer or operating system software. Alternatively, you can refer to any of the many fine books on the subject such as *IBM PC: An Introduction to the Operating System,*

In PCL commands, the number one = 1; the lowercase letter "el" = l; the number zero = Ø; and the uppercase letter "oh" = O.

BASIC Programming, and Applications, by Larry Joel Goldstein, published by Brady.

The essential BASIC command instructing your computer to transmit data to the printer is `LPRINT`. This command transmits the characters following it on same the line. The characters to be transmitted must be contained in quotes, as in "`ABC`" or "`&l1ØE`". Once again, though, we run into the problem of determining how to tell BASIC to transmit the Escape character. Fortunately, BASIC provides a simple technique. We can describe any ASCII character by its decimal representation using the command:

```
CHR$(XXX)
```

where `XXX` is the decimal ASCII number of the character (use the table in Appendix D to convert characters to ASCII decimal values). As mentioned earlier, the Escape character has the ASCII value 027. So we can transmit the Escape character as follows:

```
1ØØ  LPRINT CHR$(Ø27)
```

Note that every line in a BASIC program needs a number (`1ØØ` in this example). You can start with any number, but it is advisable to allow a gap between line numbers, in case you have to add lines later. We'll start with 100 and proceed in increments of 100. This permits additions before and after any given command line. Following the line number is the command (`LPRINT`) and the object of that Command (`CHR$(Ø27)`). You can place more than one object of the `LPRINT` command on a single line with a single `LPRINT` command, by separating the objects with a semicolon ;. Thus, to transmit the printer reset command, ^{E}c`E`, use the following BASIC command:

```
1ØØ  LPRINT    CHR$(Ø27);"E";
```

(Note that the Escape code must begin each line and a semicolon must end each line except the last in a given program. The terminal semicolon suppresses the automatic carriage return and line feed sent by BASIC at the end of each line.) To transmit the font selec-

In PCL commands, the number one = 1; the lowercase letter "el" = l; the number zero = Ø; and the uppercase letter "oh" = O.

tion command described earlier, ^{E}c&l0O^{E}c(8U^{E}c(s1p10v0s3b5T, use the following command:

```
100  LPRINT    CHR$(027);"&l0O";
200  LPRINT    CHR$(027);"(8U";
300  LPRINT    CHR$(027);"(s1p10v0s3b5T"
```

which takes the three components of the font change command and sends them sequentially to the printer.

Now let's try a BASIC program that doesn't depend on your having a particular font available. This will allow you to enter the command as listed here, test the results, and see for yourself how easy it is to send PCL printer language commands to your LaserJet. We'll transmit the command we described on page 55 to set the left margin to one inch, which will give you sufficient space to hole punch your documents. Here's how you'd do that:

1. Start BASIC by typing

   ```
   BASIC
   ```

   from your DOS prompt (C: for hard-disk users or A: for floppy-disk users). If you are using an IBM clone, you may have to insert the diskette containing the BASIC interpreter (program), BASIC.COM, in drive A:. You will be presented with a blank screen, a headline across the top, a listing of the function keys across the bottom, and a cursor located in the upper-left corner underneath the BASIC prompt, `Ok` (see Figure 2.2).
2. Carefully type the command:

   ```
   100 LPRINT CHR$(027);"&a12L"
   ```

   Be sure that the spacing and use of upper- and lowercase letters is absolutely correct. Press **<RETURN>** at the end of the line. If necessary, you can retype it or use the BASIC editing commands. (See your BASIC manual).

In PCL commands, the number one = 1; the lowercase letter "el" = l; the number zero = 0; and the uppercase letter "oh" = O.

3. After you are certain you have typed the command correctly, press the RUN key **<F2>** on the IBM PC, or type the command `RUN` on a separate line and press **<RETURN>**. The program will transmit the command to the printer. Note that the Form Feed light will now be illuminated, indicating that the command was received by and is stored in the printer's memory, which will await the rest of the page data before printing.

```
The IBM Personal Computer Basic
Version A3.30 Copyright IBM Corp. 1981, 1982, 1983, 1984, 1985, 1986, 1987
60225 Bytes free

Ok

_
















1LIST  2RUN←  3LOAD"  4SAVE"  5CONT←  6,"LPT1  7TRON←  8TROFF←  9KEY  0SCREEN
```

Figure 2.2 The screen after loading BASIC.

4. Before you exit BASIC, you should save the PCL command program that you have just created for future use. This is done by entering the BASIC command:

   `SAVE"filename`

   where filename is an appropriate file name of up to eight characters (a shortcut for entering the word `SAVE"` is to

In PCL commands, the number one = `1`; the lowercase letter "el" = `l`; the number zero = `Ø`; and the uppercase letter "oh" = `O`.

press the **<F4>** key). BASIC will automatically add the .BAS extension. For our one-inch margin example, save it as MARGIN1 by entering

```
SAVE"MARGIN1
```

The file will be stored on the default drive as `MARGIN1.BAS`. Now you can execute the program by loading it by name and running it.

5. Confirm that you have actually changed the margin by switching back to DOS and typing

```
SYSTEM
```

and pressing **<RETURN>**. At the DOS prompt, type **DIR** and press **<RETURN>** to list the current directory. With the screen still full of data, press and hold the **<SHIFT>** key and press the **<PRTSC>** key. This will cause the current screen to be printed. If your BASIC command was properly entered, you should see a perfect one-inch left margin; if not, your file listings will be printed out with the LaserJet's default quarter-inch margin.

> **Note:** The print screen utility only prints 25 lines of data. Since the LaserJet waits for a full page before printing, you will have to eject the page manually by pressing the **ONLINE** button and then pressing the **FORM FEED** button. Press the **ONLINE** button to return the printer to the Ready state. Alternatively, you could send the PCL page eject command, `Ec&l0H`. The BASIC program would be:
>
> ```
> 100    LPRINT    CHR$(27);"&l0H"
> ```

In PCL commands, the number one = `1`; the lowercase letter "el" = `l`; the number zero = `0`; and the uppercase letter "oh" = `O`.

Batch Files and BASIC

Since BASIC is always available to IBM PC users (the program is actually stored on ROM chips in the computer), it is the language most easily used for quick setup of PCL commands. The only problem with BASIC is that it has to be loaded, executed, and unloaded each time you want to issue the command. In order to facilitate this process, we recommend creating a *batch file* that will execute each BASIC program you write for your printer. Batch files are short programs written with DOS commands, and are used primarily to start other programs such as the aforementioned BASIC program. Batch programs can both load and run a named BASIC program. The BASIC program can then be modified to unload itself.

Before creating a batch file to run the MARGIN1.BAS program we wrote above for setting the left margin to one inch, it's necessary to make one minor adjustment to MARGIN.BAS. The adjustment allows the batch file to return to DOS when it is done. The following steps accomplish this purpose:

1. Start BASIC by typing

   ```
   BASIC <RETURN>
   ```

   at the DOS prompt.
2. Load MARGIN1.BAS by typing

   ```
   LOAD"MARGIN1 <RETURN>
   ```

3. Add another line by typing

   ```
   999 SYSTEM <RETURN>
   ```

   This will add the command to return to DOS at the end of the program. (Note: you can use whatever number you like to precede `SYSTEM`, as long as it's the highest numbered line of your program).
4. Save the new version by typing:

   ```
   SAVE"MARGIN1 <RETURN>
   ```

In PCL commands, the number one = `1`; the lowercase letter "el" = `l`; the number zero = `Ø`; and the uppercase letter "oh" = `O`.

5. Exit BASIC by typing the command:

```
SYSTEM <RETURN>
```

Now we're ready to create the batch file for running MARGIN1. In this example, we'll use the **DOS COPY CON** command, which creates the batch program file by copying the data entered from the keyboard (CON = Console = Keyboard) directly to a disk file. You could also use the EDLIN editor or your favorite word processor in ASCII mode to create the batch file, but for such simple tasks the DOS COPY CON command is the quickest and easiest. Start the process of creating a batch file by typing:

```
COPY CON MARGIN1.BAT <RETURN>
```

Note the use of the spacial .BAT extension. You must now enter the text of the file very carefully. If you make an error, you will have to start again. Type:

```
BASIC MARGIN1
```

Then press

```
<CTRL><F6>
```

This will cause the character **^Z** to appear at the end of the file and the system will display:

```
1 File Copied
```

That's all there is to creating a batch file.

You are now ready to test your new Batch file/BASIC program combination. Simply type:

```
MARGIN1 <RETURN>
```

at the DOS prompt. The Batch file will start BASIC and execute the MARGIN1.BAS program, which will in turn return control to DOS and leave you back at the DOS prompt. Check to see that your program worked by using the directory printing test described above. By using MARGIN1.BAT and MARGIN1.BAS as models, you can now create Batch/BASIC program combinations for all your PCL printer language command needs.

Issuing PCL Printer Language Commands from Application Software

Most major word processing, database, and spreadsheet programs provide a method for transmitting printer codes directly to the printer. In some cases, you must completely convert each character of the command to its ASCII representation. In others, you only need to convert those characters that can't otherwise be transmitted with the Escape character.

dBASE III Plus

PCL printer language commands can be used from within *dBASE* to format pages, change fonts, and carry out other printer functions. For example, to set the left margin command in *dBASE III Plus*, issue the following sequence of commands:

```
SET PRINTER ON
?? CHR(027)+"&a12L"
```

where the first line directs unformatted display output to the printer as well as the screen. The ?? in the second line instructs the computer to transmit the subsequent characters to the printer without issuing a line feed. As with BASIC, dBASE uses a special command to transmit the Escape character. dBASE uses the function `CHR(XXX)` to create the ASCII character represented by the decimal `XXX`. dBASE then uses the plus sign + to concatenate the ASCII Escape character with the rest of the PCL printer language command string.

In PCL commands, the number one = 1; the lowercase letter "el" = l; the number zero = 0; and the uppercase letter "oh" = O.

Lotus 1-2-3

Lotus 1-2-3 uses the backslash character \ to indicate that an ASCII code will follow. To issue the same margin command, we could either insert it into the printer setup string as a *global* command (i.e., a printer setup that applies to the whole worksheet), or we could issue it as an embedded in-line print command (i.e., a command that applies only to a header or a portion of the worksheet) by using the print prefix, `||`.

A sample global command for changing to Landscape, Line Printer (compressed) Print is input as follows. Type:

`\PPOS` (which stands for Print Printer Option Setup)

1-2-3 will prompt you in the menu bar area atop the worksheet with the prompt `Enter setup string:`. Type

```
\027E\027&l1o2e5.647c66F\027&k2S
```

and then press the **<RETURN>** key followed by **<ESC>QAG**.

The worksheet will then print out in Landscape orientation, using the compressed line printer type font, provided the font is available on a cartridge, a soft font, or internally with the LaserJet Series II printer.

An inline print command is used to highlight a particular area of a worksheet. Perhaps you want the worksheet to print with a 14 point Helvetica bold title. Insert the font selection command

```
||\027l0O\027(0U\027(s1p14.4v0s3b4T
```

in the leftmost cell of the line preceding the headline. The first vertical bar is treated as a label prefix and will not show on the worksheet. You also need to reset the printer to its default font after the title. Do this using the same type of embedded command. To reset to Courier 10 point type, enter:

```
||\027l0O\027(8U\027s0p10h12v0s0b3T
```

In PCL commands, the number one = 1; the lowercase letter "el" = l; the number zero = 0; and the uppercase letter "oh" = O.

in the leftmost cell of the line after the title.

One of the most important embedded print commands for 1-2-3 is the page eject command. This allows you to explicitly control where the page breaks will occur in a long worksheet without having to insert and delete dummy spacing lines. To force 1-2-3 to break a page at a particular line, enter the command:

```
::\Ø27&lØH
```

on the line after the last line you want to print on the current page.

Typing such long strings of characters is often difficult and always boring. Section I describes how to use Lotus Macros and the enclosed diskette to facilitate entering 1-2-3 setup strings and embedded print commands.

WordPerfect 4.2

WordPerfect also provides the feature to transmit PCL codes directly to the printer, although installing the correct print driver will greatly reduce the need to transmit individual PCL codes. Nevertheless, there are some occasions, such as when selecting soft fonts for which WordPerfect has no drivers, that will necessitate the use of the PCL printer language. To access the Printer Command feature of WordPerfect, press

```
<CTRL><F8>
```

and select option A from the menu. The prompt

```
Cmnd:
```

will appear at the bottom of the screen. Enter the PCL printer language command using angled brackets **< >** to mark characters that are being sent as ASCII codes, such as **<027>** for Escape. To select a special headline font, such as Time Roman 36-point type

---

In PCL commands, the number one = 1; the lowercase letter "el" = l; the number zero = Ø; and the uppercase letter "oh" = O.

downloaded from one of the HP soft font disks, insert the command:

```
Cmnd: <027>&l0O<027>(8U<027>(s1p36v0s3b5T
```

before the headline. Bear in mind that you now need to reset the printer to the default font after the headline by using a printer command corresponding to the body type.

Other Application Programs

Just about all application packages have their own syntax and coding rules for issuing printer control commands. The three examples listed above demonstrate some of the common techniques. You should refer to the printer setup or command section of your software manual for more information about transmitting printer commands.

If your software doesn't support direct transmission of printer control commands, don't do anything rash—you are not totally without a paddle. You can usually transmit the necessary commands via BASIC prior to starting the application. You should be aware, however, that some applications automatically send a printer reset upon startup. This will undo whatever PCL printer language codes you have transmitted through BASIC. In some cases you can avoid the printer reset of these recalcitrant programs by turning your printer offline while the application is loading and then turning it back online, so the reset command has been transmitted into oblivion.

You can also use one of the many RAM resident laser printer utilities that either specifically support PCL printer language commands or allow you to issue your own PCL commands after you have started your application. (A number of these utilities are listed in the Software and Hardware Solutions directory, part number 5954-8969D, supplied free from Hewlett-Packard. The directory is updated periodically, and contains listings for hundreds of programs that support or enhance the LaserJet.)

Raster Graphics

PCL can transmit graphic images to the printer as strings of data that represent the image to be printed as series of zeroes and ones. These are called *raster* or *bit-mapped images*. As the laser beam is scanned across the image, it is pulsed on and off corresponding to the dots that make up the image. The instruction to pulse the laser on for a dot is 1 while the Øs represent the white areas of the image. Figure 2.3 shows how an arrow is represented as a raster graphic.

Dot Row	Binary Representation			
	Byte 1	Byte 2	Byte 3	Byte 4
1	00000000	00000000	10000000	00000000
2	00000000	00000000	11000000	00000000
3	00000000	00000000	11100000	00000000
4	00000000	00000000	11110000	00000000
5	00000000	00000000	11111000	00000000
6	00000000	00000000	11111100	00000000
7	00000000	00000000	11111110	00000000
8	00000000	00000000	11111111	00000000
9	00000000	00000000	11111111	10000000
10	11111111	11111111	11111111	11000000
11	11111111	11111111	11111111	11100000
12	11111111	11111111	11111111	11110000
13	11111111	11111111	11111111	11111000
14	11111111	11111111	11111111	11111100
15	11111111	11111111	11111111	11111110
16	11111111	11111111	11111111	11111111
17	11111111	11111111	11111111	11111111
18	11111111	11111111	11111111	11111110
19	11111111	11111111	11111111	11111100
20	11111111	11111111	11111111	11111000
21	11111111	11111111	11111111	11110000
22	11111111	11111111	11111111	11100000
23	11111111	11111111	11111111	11000000
24	00000000	00000000	11111111	10000000
25	00000000	00000000	11111111	00000000
26	00000000	00000000	11111110	00000000
27	00000000	00000000	11111100	00000000
28	00000000	00000000	11111000	00000000
29	00000000	00000000	11110000	00000000
30	00000000	00000000	11100000	00000000
31	00000000	00000000	11000000	00000000
32	00000000	00000000	10000000	00000000

Figure 2.3 Raster or bit mapped image of an arrow

You must perform several steps to send a raster graphic image to the printer. First, you must tell the printer where to start the image. Second, you must tell the printer what resolution the data will represent. The printer always prints with 300 DPI resolution, but you can send data that are lower in resolution and the printer will automatically translate them to a 300 DPI representation. The image will appear coarser since each dot of data sent to the printer is printed as a fixed pattern of 300 DPI dots set according to the resolution (see Figure 2.4). For example, a 150 DPI resolution image uses a pattern of four dots printed for every data point, while a 75 DPI resolution image uses a pattern of 16 dots for each data point. The chief advantage of using lower resolution images is that they require less user memory. For example, a two-inch by three-inch image at 75 DPI resolution requires 34,200 bits of user memory, while the same image at 300 DPI requires 540,000 bits.

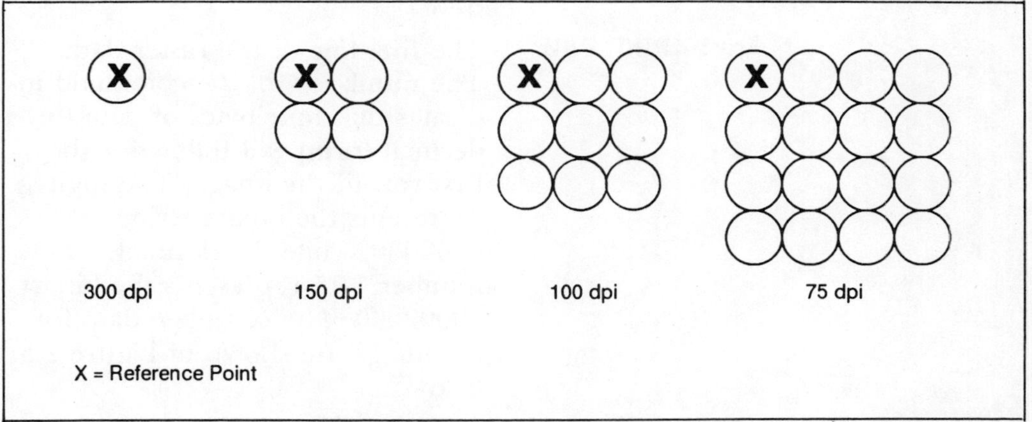

Figure 2.4 Dot pattern for each data point at various resolutions.

The third step in the process of sending a raster graphic image is to define the left margin, either as the current position or as the left edge of the Logical Page. In most cases you would want to position the cursor in the appropriate location for the upper-left corner of the image and define the left margin of the image as the current location. The fourth step is to send the actual data. As with all raster

In PCL commands, the number one = `1`; the lowercase letter "el" = `l`; the number zero = `Ø`; and the uppercase letter "oh" = `O`.

data, the command preceding each line of the data contains information describing how many bytes of data will be following. While the image is most easily seen in terms of binary data, the command is actually sent using the decimal equivalent of the data. For example, the binary byte 00000000 is represented as 0, while the string 10000000 is 128 and the string 11111111 is 255. The final step is to indicate the end of the raster data.

To send the arrow image contained in Figure 2.3, use the following series of commands:

1. ^{E}c*p300x400Y — Positions the cursor at coordinates 300,400 on the page.
2. ^{E}c*t75R — Sets the resolution to 75 DPI.
3. ^{E}c*r1A — Sets the left graphics margin at the current position, i.e., 300 dots from the left edge of the page as set in step 1.
4. ^{E}c*b4W001280 — The first line of the raster data. The number 4 in the command indicates that four bytes of data (in decimal form) will follow for the first row of the image. The digit 0 represents the binary string 0000000, while the decimal number 128 represents the binary 10000000. The complete data for the image are shown in Figure 2.5 below.
5. ^{E}c*rB — Indicates the end of the raster data.

The completed image as it would be printed is shown in Figure 2.6.

While this seems extremely complicated, it is usually handled automatically by your software. When you install software with the correct driver for use with the HP LaserJet, you are telling the software how to transmit graphic data to the printer. Thereafter, the software will generate the necessary command strings to transmit its images to the printer. The only time that you might need to send

---

In PCL commands, the number one = 1; the lowercase letter "el" = l; the number zero = 0; and the uppercase letter "oh" = O.

graphics data to the printer manually would be if you wanted to create a unique logo for your company or product. This image could be inserted whenever and wherever you wished using the above procedure.

Dot Row	byte 1	byte 2	byte 3	byte 4	Decimal Equivalent*
1	00000000	00000000	10000000	00000000	Ec*b4W[0, 0, 128, 0]
2	00000000	00000000	11000000	00000000	Ec*b4W[0, 0, 192, 0]
3	00000000	00000000	11100000	00000000	Ec*b4W[0, 0, 224, 0]
4	00000000	00000000	11110000	00000000	Ec*b4W[0, 0, 240, 0]
5	00000000	00000000	11111000	00000000	Ec*b4W[0, 0, 248, 0]
6	00000000	00000000	11111100	00000000	Ec*b4W[0, 0, 252, 0]
7	00000000	00000000	11111110	00000000	Ec*b4W[0, 0, 254, 0]
8	00000000	00000000	11111111	00000000	Ec*b4W[0, 0, 255, 0]
9	00000000	00000000	11111111	10000000	Ec*b4W[0, 0, 255, 128]
10	11111111	11111111	11111111	11000000	Ec*b4W[255, 255, 255, 192]
11	11111111	11111111	11111111	11100000	Ec*b4W[255, 255, 255, 224]
12	11111111	11111111	11111111	11110000	Ec*b4W[255, 255, 255, 240]
13	11111111	11111111	11111111	11111000	Ec*b4W[255, 255, 255, 248]
14	11111111	11111111	11111111	11111100	Ec*b4W[255, 255, 255, 252]
15	11111111	11111111	11111111	11111110	Ec*b4W[255, 255, 255, 254]
16	11111111	11111111	11111111	11111111	Ec*b4W[255, 255, 255, 255]
17	11111111	11111111	11111111	11111111	Ec*b4W[255, 255, 255, 255]
18	11111111	11111111	11111111	11111110	Ec*b4W[255, 255, 255, 254]
19	11111111	11111111	11111111	11111100	Ec*b4W[255, 255, 255, 252]
20	11111111	11111111	11111111	11111000	Ec*b4W[255, 255, 255, 248]
21	11111111	11111111	11111111	11110000	Ec*b4W[255, 255, 255, 240]
22	11111111	11111111	11111111	11100000	Ec*b4W[255, 255, 255, 224]
23	11111111	11111111	11111111	11000000	Ec*b4W[255, 255, 255, 192]
24	00000000	00000000	11111111	10000000	Ec*b4W[0, 0, 255, 128]
25	00000000	00000000	11111111	00000000	Ec*b4W[0, 0, 255, 0]
26	00000000	00000000	11111110	00000000	Ec*b4W[0, 0, 254, 0]
27	00000000	00000000	11111100	00000000	Ec*b4W[0, 0, 252, 0]
28	00000000	00000000	11111000	00000000	Ec*b4W[0, 0, 248, 0]
29	00000000	00000000	11110000	00000000	Ec*b4W[0, 0, 240, 0]
30	00000000	00000000	11100000	00000000	Ec*b4W[0, 0, 224, 0]
31	00000000	00000000	11000000	00000000	Ec*b4W[0, 0, 192, 0]
32	00000000	00000000	10000000	00000000	Ec*b4W[0, 0, 128, 0]
	Raster Image				Raster Data Commands

* The brackets and commas are not part of the raster data command; they are used only to delineate the data.

Figure 2.5 Raster data for arrow.

In PCL commands, the number one = 1; the lowercase letter "el" = l; the number zero = Ø; and the uppercase letter "oh" = O.

Rectangular Fill Graphics

In addition to printing raster graphics, the HP LaserJet printers can generate and print rectangular lines and boxes with either shaded or patterned fill. To generate a shaded box or line, you must first

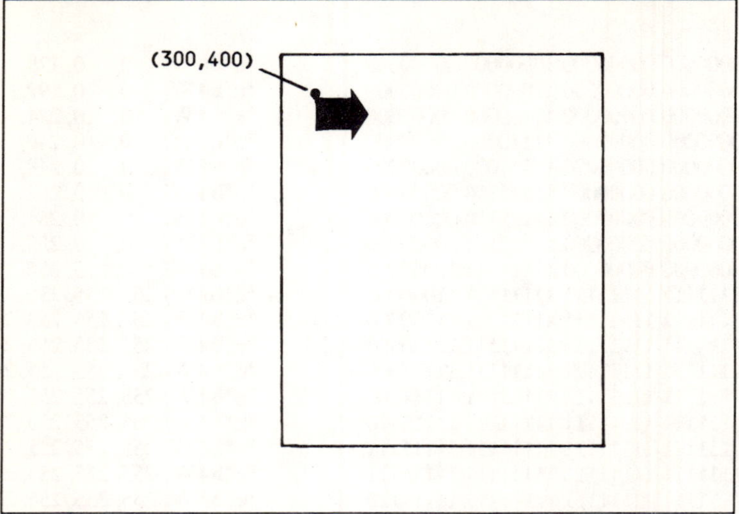

Figure 2.6 Printed image of arrow.

position the cursor in the upper-left corner of the space, using one of the positioning commands, then specify the size of the element and the type of filling, and finally issue a print command.

To position the cursor in the upper-left corner of the box or line, you can use any of the positioning commands. For example, you could specify the position by its PCL coordinates in dots. To position the element starting at location 300,400, issue the command:

```
Ec*p300x400Y
```

To describe a rectangular graphic element such as a rule or box, you must define its shape and size by setting its horizontal and vertical dimensions relative to the current cursor position. To set a hori-

In PCL commands, the number one = 1; the lowercase letter "el" = l; the number zero = 0; and the uppercase letter "oh" = O.

zontal dimension of four inches in terms of decipoints (1/720th of an inch), first calculate the total number of decipoints as:

4″ × 720 DPI = 2880 Decipoints

and then enter the command:

```
EC*c2880H
```

To set a vertical dimension of three inches in terms of decipoints (1/720th of an inch), first calculate the total number of decipoints as:

3″ × 720 DPI = 2160 Decipoints

and then enter the command:

```
EC*c2160V
```

You can also specify the size in terms of dots. The same four-inch by three-inch box could be specified with the commands:

4″ × 300 DPI = 1200 Dots
```
EC*c1200A
```
3″ × 300 DPI = 900 Dots
```
EC*c900B
```

The next step involves setting the fill pattern or shading. The shading is set as a percentage from 1 to 100. One of eight specific shadings will be assigned based on the value specified, as shown in Figure 2.7. The fill patterns are assigned by selecting a number from 1 to 6 corresponding to the patterns shown in Figure 2.8.

You will notice that the fill pattern numbers and the possible percentage numbers overlap. The specific option will be resolved when you specify the type of fill to be used in the final draw command. To select a fill pattern of vertical lines (pattern #2), use the following command:

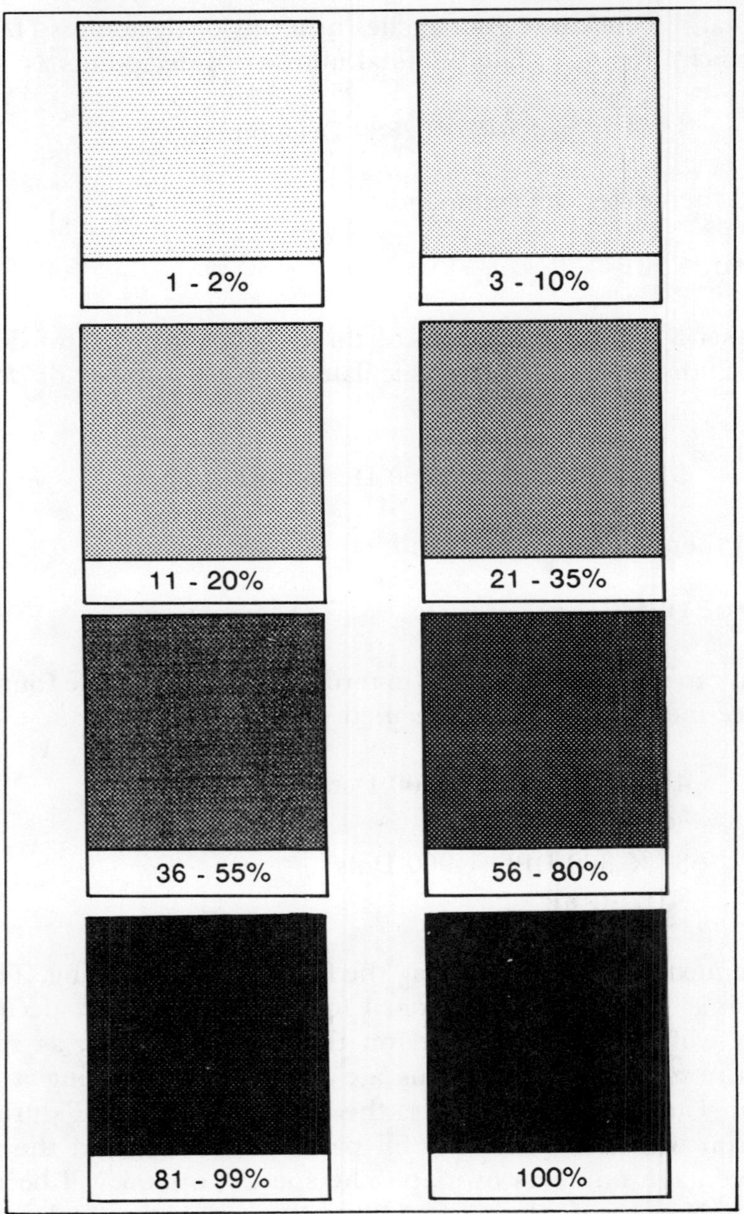

Figure 2.7 Rectangular fill graphics—shading levels.

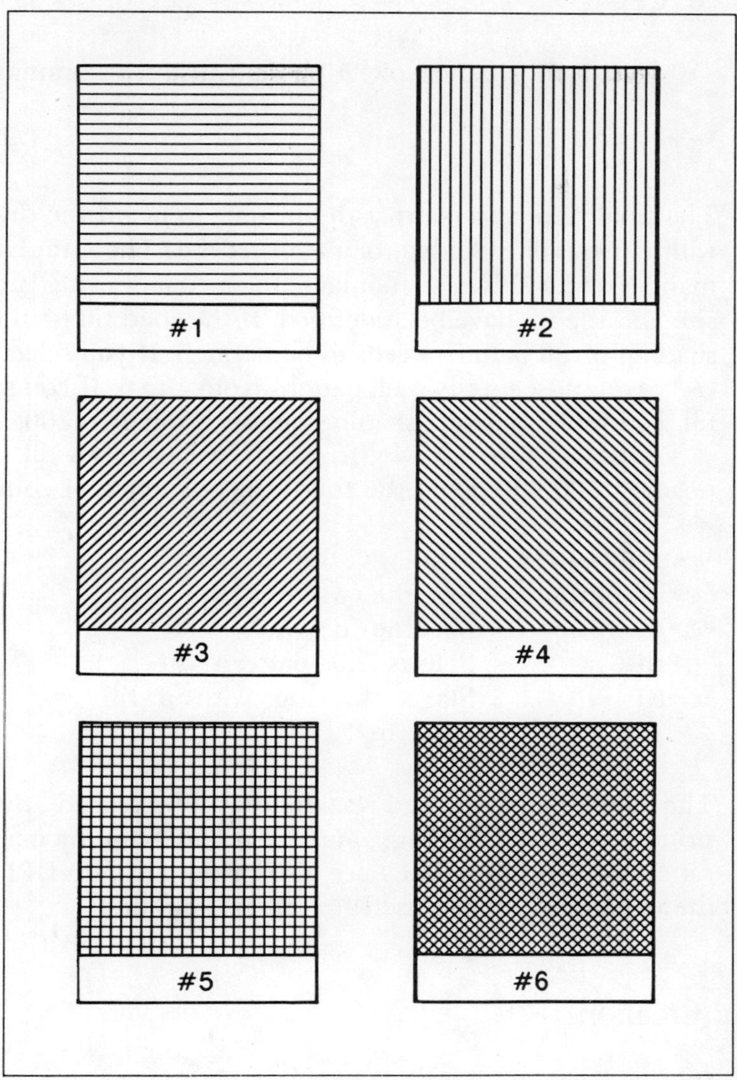

Figure 2.8 Rectangular fill graphics—fill patterns.

In PCL commands, the number one = 1; the lowercase letter "el" = l; the number zero = Ø; and the uppercase letter "oh" = O.

```
Ec*c2G
```

To select a fill shading of 25 percent, use the command:

```
Ec*c25G
```

The final step is to instruct the printer to begin the drawing process with either solid, shaded, or patterned fill. The Graphics-Draw command (Ec*c#P) is used to initiate the actual drawing process after the size and the fill have been defined. If the solid fill (#0) is selected, no shading or fill pattern needs to be defined. If you select patterned fill (#3), you must specify a fill pattern from 1 to 6. If you select a shaded fill, you must specify a shading density from 1 to 100.

To draw a four-inch by five-inch box with #5 fill pattern at the position 700,900, issue the following sequence of commands:

Ec*p700x900Y	Positions the cursor
Ec*c1200A	Set the width
Ec*c1500B	Set the height
Ec*c6G	Selects fill pattern #6
Ec*3P	Starts drawing with a fill pattern

The shaded or patterned rectangles can be placed anywhere on the printable area of the page, and are not affected by margin or perforation skip settings. They are also printed at 300 DPI regardless of the resolution setting used for raster graphics.

Soft Font Creation

While most users will find it easier to purchase soft fonts from HP or one of the many font designers, others may find it necessary to create special fonts or characters. With the PCL printer language, it is possible to create and download individual characters or even complete fonts. Creating a soft font requires several steps. The first takes place before you turn your computer on and involves designing the individ-

In PCL commands, the number one = 1; the lowercase letter "el" = l; the number zero = 0; and the uppercase letter "oh" = O.

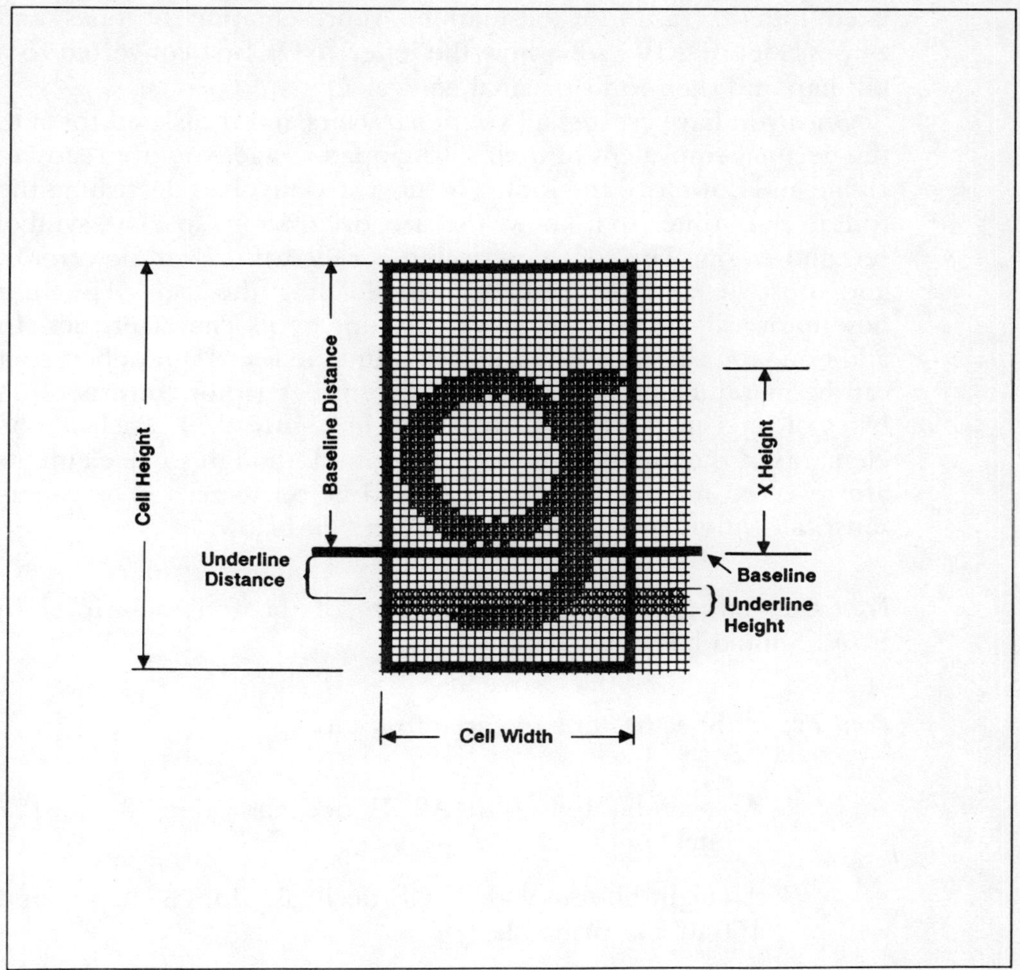

Figure 2.9 Soft font design grid.

ual characters on a 300 DPI grid (see Figure 2.9). The individual characters must be of the same general size and are drawn within a rectangular cell that must be the same size for all characters in the font. The cell size defines the size of the printed characters and is specified in the number of dots at 300 dots per inch.

In PCL commands, the number one = 1; the lowercase letter "el" = l; the number zero = 0; and the uppercase letter "oh" = O.

After drawing each character in its cell, the image must be translated into its raster or bit-mapped representation of ones and zeroes. Figure 2.10 shows how the letter "g" is first converted to a bit map and then to its decimal equivalent.

Once you have created all your characters and translated them to the decimal equivalent of their bit-mapped image, you are ready to create and download the font. The next step involves describing the font to the printer so it knows the size, orientation, spacing, symbol set, and so on. The font description is called the *Font Descriptor*, and must be declared prior to downloading the font. The font descriptor will be used to select the font by its characteristics. In addition, you should assign the font a unique font ID number, so it can be manipulated by number. The font descriptor consists of 64 bytes of data in the format described in Figure 2.11. Each of the elements of the font descriptor are required, though some elements are reserved for future use and should be set to zero. The others must fall within specific ranges as described below.

Font Descriptor Size: Declares the size of the font descriptor in bytes. Should be set to 64.

Font Type: Specifies one of three font types:

0 A seven-bit font with ASCII decimal values 32 to 127 printable.

1 An eight-bit font with ASCII decimal values 32 to 127 and 160 to 255 printable.

2 PC-8 font with all characters printable except ASCII decimal values 0, 7–15, and 27.

Baseline Distance: The measure from the top of the character cell to the imaginary line running along the bottom of each character (excluding the descenders of some characters). The legal values are 0 to one dot less than the cell height.

Dot Row	Bit Map	Decimal Equivalent			
01	00000000 11111100 00001111 1100000	0	252	15	192
02	00000111 11111111 00011111 1110000	7	255	31	224
03	00001111 11111111 10011111 1100000	15	225	159	192
04	00111111 11010111 11011110 0000000	63	219	224	0
05	00111110 00000001 11111110 0000000	62	1	254	0
06	01111100 00000000 01111110 0000000	124	0	126	0
07	01111000 00000000 01111110 0000000	120	0	126	0
08	11110000 00000000 00111110 0000000	240	0	62	0
09	11110000 00000000 00111110 0000000	240	0	62	0
10	11110000 00000000 00011110 0000000	240	0	30	0
11	11110000 00000000 00011110 0000000	240	0	30	0
12	11110000 00000000 00011110 0000000	240	0	30	0
13	11110000 00000000 00011110 0000000	240	0	30	0
14	11110000 00000000 00111110 0000000	240	0	62	0
15	01111000 00000000 00111110 0000000	120	0	62	0
16	01111000 00000000 01111110 0000000	120	0	126	0
17	01111100 00000000 11111110 0000000	124	0	254	0
18	00111110 00000001 11111110 0000000	62	1	254	0
19	00011111 11010111 11011110 0000000	31	219	222	0
20	00001111 11111111 10011110 0000000	15	255	158	0
21	00000111 11111111 00011110 0000000	7	255	30	0
22	00000000 10101000 00011110 0000000	0	172	30	0
23	00000000 00000000 00011110 0000000	0	0	30	0
24	00000000 00000000 00011110 0000000	0	0	30	0
25	00000000 00000000 00011110 0000000	0	0	30	0
26	00000000 00000000 00111110 0000000	0	0	62	0
27	00000000 00000000 00111100 0000000	0	0	60	0
28	00000000 00000000 01111100 0000000	0	0	124	0
29	00000000 00000001 11111000 0000000	0	1	248	0
30	00000001 11111111 11110000 0000000	1	255	240	0
31	00000011 11111111 11100000 0000000	3	255	224	0
32	00000001 11111111 10000000 0000000	1	255	128	0

Figure 2.10 Bit mapped image of letter "g."

Cell Width: The width of the character cell used to declare the size of the characters of the font. The value must lie between 0 and 4200.

Byte	15 - MSB 8	7 LSB - 0
0	Font descriptor Size	
2	Reserved	Font Type
4	Reserved	
6	Baseline Distance	
8	Cell Width	
10	Cell Height	
12	Orientation	Spacing
14	Symbol Set	
16	Pitch (Default HMI)	
18	Height	
20	xHeight	
22	Width Type	Style
24	Stroke Weight	Typeface
26	Reserved	Serif Style
28	Reserved	
30	Underline Distance	Underline Height
32	Text Height	
34	Text Width	
36	Reserved	
38	Reserved	
40	Pitch Extended	Height Extended
42	Reserved	
44	Reserved	
46	Reserved	
48-63	Font Name	

Figure 2.11 Font descriptor format.

Cell Height: The height of the character cell used to declare the size of the characters of the font. The value must lie between 0 and 4200.

Orientation: Declares the orientation of the font as either Portrait (lengthwise) or Landscape (widthwise). The value must be either 0 for Portrait or 1 for Landscape.

Spacing: Either fixed spacing (0) or proportional spacing (1).

Symbol Set: Declares the symbol set that will be used for the font. The actual number must lie between 0 and 2047, with 0 to 1023 reserved for use by HP, and 1024 through 2047 available for independent font developers. The value of the symbol set is determined by a complex formula based on its PCL escape sequence value field and terminal character, and is determined by multiplying the value field by 32, adding the ASCII decimal value of the terminal character, and subtracting 64. The common symbol sets and their values are listed in Table 2.1.

Pitch: Specifies the pitch of the font in units equal to one-quarter of a dot (i.e., 1200 per inch). The pitch defines the default Horizontal Motion Index (HMI) for the font and can be set to any value between 0 and 16800.

Height: Specifies the height of the font in units equal to one-quarter of a dot (i.e., 1200 per inch). The height defines the default Vertical Motion Index (VMI) for the font and can be set to any value between 0 and 10922. When converted to points (1/72 of an inch), this is the common measure of the size of a font.

xHeight: Specifies the body height of the characters as measured by the height of the lowercase letter "x". This is entered in units equal to one-quarter dot (i.e., 1200 per inch).

Width Type: Used to describe the general proportional width of the characters from condensed to expanded. This is not used by the LaserJet Series II printer.

Style: Describes the slant of the characters of the font. A value of 0 indicates upright or Roman, while a value of 1 indicates italics.

Table 2.1 Common symbol sets.

Symbol Set Name	PCL Value Field	PCL Termination Character	Symbol Set Value
HP Math-7	0	A	1
HP Line Draw	0	B	2
ISO 60: Norwegian version 1	0	D	4
ISO 61: Norwegian version 2	1	D	36
HP Roman Extensions	0	E	5
ISO 4: United Kingdom	1	E	37
ISO 25: French	0	F	6
ISO 69: French	1	F	38
HP German	0	G	7
ISO 21: German	1	G	39
HP Greek-8	8	G	263
ISO 15: Italian	0	I	9
ISO 14: JIS ASCII	0	K	11
ISO 57: Chinese	2	K	75
Technical-7	1	M	45
HP Math-8	8	M	269
ISO 100: ECMA-94 (Latin 1)	0	N	14
OCR A	0	O	15
OCR B	1	O	47
ISO 11: Swedish	0	S	19
HP Spanish	1	S	51
ISO 17: Spanish	2	S	83
ISO 10: Spanish	3	S	115
ISO 16: Portuguese	4	S	147
ISO 84: Portuguese	5	S	179
ISO 85: Spanish	6	S	211
ISO 6: ASCII	0	U	21
HP Legal	1	U	53
ISO 2: Intl Reference Version	2	U	85
OEM-1	7	U	245
HP Roman-8	8	U	277
PC-8	10	U	341
PC-8 (D/N)	11	U	373
HP Pi Font	15	U	501

Stroke Weight: Specifies the thickness of the strokes used to form the characters of the font. The weight can vary from −7 to 7, with −7 representing the thinnest strokes and 7 representing the boldest. The most commonly used values are −3 for light weight, 0 for medium, and 3 for bold.

Type Face: Specifies one of the predefined typefaces. HP assigns specific values to its own and third-party faces. The list is dynamic, and additional values will be specified in the future. Current values are shown in Table 2.2.

Serif Style: Specifies one of the predefined serif styles, from sans serif rounded to serif block and many others. This field is ignored by the LaserJet Series II.

Underline Distance: Specifies the distance from the baseline of the font to the position for underlining the characters. The distance is measured to the top line of dots of the underline and is measured in dots. Positive values place the underline above the baseline, while negative values place it below the baseline.

Underline Height: Describes the vertical thickness of the underline stroke in dots. The LaserJet always uses three-dot thick underlines and ignores this field.

Text Height: Specifies the interline spacing of the font in units of one-quater of a dot. This field is ignored by the LaserJet Series II printer.

Text Width: Specifies the average horizontal width of a lower-case character in the font. This field is ignored by the LaserJet Series II printer.

Font Name: A 16-character name that can be used by some software to show what fonts are available. This name is also displayed by the LaserJet Series II printer in its Font Sample Printout.

Table 2.2 Common type faces.

Value	Typeface
0	Line Printer
3	Courier
4	Helv
5	TmsRmn
6	Letter Gothic
8	Prestige
11	Presentations
17	Optima
18	Garamond
19	Cooper Black
20	Coronet Bold
21	Broadway
22	Bauer Bodoni Black Condensed
23	Century Schoolbook
24	University Roman

Pitch Extended: This field is used as an addition to the pitch field, and fine-tunes the pitch. It is measured in 1/1024ths of a single dot, giving it extreme precision. The final font pitch is equal to the sum of the pitch and the pitch-extended fields.

Height Extended: This field is used as an addition to the height field and is used to fine-tune the font height. This field is measured in 1/1024ths of a single dot, giving it extreme precision. The final font height is equal to the sum of the height and the height-extended fields.

To send a font descriptor for a font about to be downloaded, first declare the font ID number with the command:

`EC*c#D` where # is the font ID number

Then send the actual 64-byte font descriptor with the command:

`EC)s64W data`

In PCL commands, the number one = 1; the lowercase letter "el" = l; the number zero = 0; and the uppercase letter "oh" = O.

where the data are the 64 bytes of the font descriptor. For example, to download the font descriptor for a Courier 10 pitch Portrait font (upright, medium, 12 point, HP Roman-8) with the ID number 3, use the command:

```
Ec*c3D
Ec)s64W data
```

where the data of the font descriptor appear in Table 2.3 below.

Now you are ready to transmit the actual character data. The first step is to tell the printer which character is to be sent. This is accomplished by assigning each character a character code, generally the ASCII decimal value assigned to that character, though the specific code assigned is up to you. The command to assign a character code is:

`Ec*c#E` where # is the code to be assigned

The next step is to describe the individual character in much the same fashion that you described the font in general above. This is done by sending a Character Descriptor command followed by the data of the descriptor and finally the bit-mapped data of the character itself. The Character Descriptor consists of specific fields, as shown in Figure 2.12. Like the font descriptor, each field has defined meanings and designated ranges of allowable values.

Format: Specifies the format of the descriptor and the data following. The value used by the LaserJet Series II printer is 4.

Continuation: Since the PCL printer language escape sequences are limited to 32,767 bits of data per block of data transmitted, large characters must be sent in more than one block of data. This is accomplished by sending a single character descriptor with the first block of data and preceding the subsequent blocks of data for the same character with a truncated descriptor that indicates that the data are a continuation of the previous block for the same character. The continuation block is shown in Figure 2.13.

Table 2.3 Sample font descriptor.

Field Name	Value	Description
Font Descriptor Size	64	
Reserved	0	
Font Type	1	8-bit
Reserved	0	
Baseline Distance	35	
Cell Width	30	
Cell Height	50	
Orientation	0	Portrait
Spacing	0	Fixed pitch
Symbol Set (8U)	277	(8*32 + (85-64))
Pitch	120	30 dots
Height	200	50 dots
x Height	92	23 dots
Width Type	0	Normal
Style	0	Upright
Stroke Weight	0	Medium
Typeface	3	Courier
Reserved	0	
Serif Style	2	Serif Line
Reserved	0	
Underline Distance	-5	
Underline Height	3	
Text Height	200	50 dots
Text Width	120	30 dots
Reserved	0	
Reserved	0	
Pitch Extended	0	
Height Extended	0	
Reserved	0	
Reserved	0	
Reserved	0	
Font Name	Courier10	

Byte	15 - MSB 8	7 LSB - 0
0	Format	Continuation
2	Descriptor Size	Class
4	Orientation	Reserved
6	Left Offset	
8	Top Offset	
10	Character Width	
12	Character Height	
14	Delta X	
16	Character Data: (in bytes) • • •	

Figure 2.12 Character descriptor format.

Byte	15 - MSB 8	7 LSB - 0
0	Format	Continuation (1)
2	Character Data: • • •	

Figure 2.13 Data continuation format.

Descriptor Size: Declares the size of the character descriptor in bytes. The LaserJet Series II uses a 14-byte descriptor.

Class: Declares the format of the character data. The LaserJet Series II printer uses the data format specified as number 1.

Orientation: Specifies the orientation of the character and must match the orientation declared for the font. Again, 0 means Portrait and 1 means Landscape.

Left Offset: Specifies the distance from the left edge of the character cell as described in the font descriptor to the leftmost edge of the actual character (see Figure 2.14). The offset is specified in dots, and can range from −4200 to 4200.

Top Offset: Specifies the distance from the baseline to the topmost point of the character (see Figure 2.14). The offset is specified in dots and can range from −4200 to 4200.

Character Width: Specifies the width of the individual character in dots up to 4200 (see Figure 2.14). Specifying an individual character width larger than the cell width declared in the font descriptor invalidates the character download.

Character Height: Specifies the height of the individual character in dots up to 4200. (See Figure 2.14). Specifying an individual character height larger than the cell height declared in the font descriptor will invalidate the character download.

Delta X: Specifies the actual horizontal cursor movement required to properly space proportional fonts. This differs from the character width in that it includes the left-off set and any space following the printed character (see Figure 2.14). The Delta X is specified in units of one-quarter of a dot from 0 to 16,800, but the LaserJet Series II printer rounds the value to the nearest whole dot.

Character Data: The decimal equivalents of the bit-mapped image in discrete bytes. The data are transmitted sequentially row by row starting in the upper-left of the character as it will be printed. Therefore, landscape characters are actually transmitted sideways, since they will be printed sideways (see Figures 2.15 and 2.16).

To download the Courier 10 pitch lowercase character "g" (12 point upright, portrait, medium) shown in Figure 2.15, send the commands:

In PCL commands, the number one = `1`; the lowercase letter "el" = `l`; the number zero = `Ø`; and the uppercase letter "oh" = `O`.

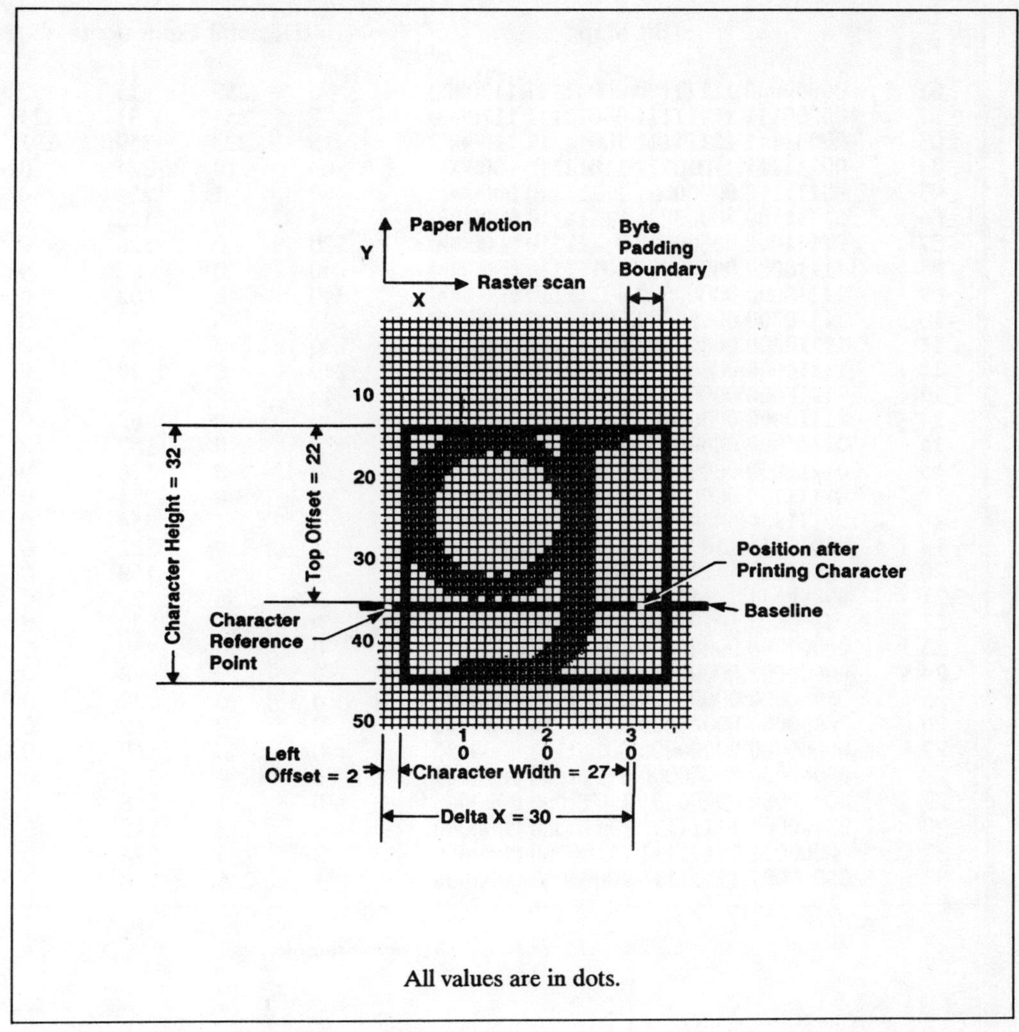

All values are in dots.

Figure 2.14 Sample character dimensions.

In PCL commands, the number one = 1; the lowercase letter "el" = l; the number zero = Ø; and the uppercase letter "oh" = O.

Dot Row	Bit Map	Decimal Equivalent			
01	00000000 11111100 00001111 1100000	0	252	15	192
02	00000111 11111111 00011111 1110000	7	255	31	224
03	00001111 11111111 10011111 1100000	15	225	159	192
04	00111111 11010111 11011110 0000000	63	219	224	0
05	00111110 00000001 11111110 0000000	62	1	254	0
06	01111100 00000000 01111110 0000000	124	0	126	0
07	01111000 00000000 01111110 0000000	120	0	126	0
08	11110000 00000000 00111110 0000000	240	0	62	0
09	11110000 00000000 00111110 0000000	240	0	62	0
10	11110000 00000000 00011110 0000000	240	0	30	0
11	11110000 00000000 00011110 0000000	240	0	30	0
12	11110000 00000000 00011110 0000000	240	0	30	0
13	11110000 00000000 00011110 0000000	240	0	30	0
14	11110000 00000000 00111110 0000000	240	0	62	0
15	01111000 00000000 00111110 0000000	120	0	62	0
16	01111000 00000000 01111110 0000000	120	0	126	0
17	01111100 00000000 11111110 0000000	124	0	254	0
18	00111110 00000001 11111110 0000000	62	1	254	0
19	00011111 11010111 11011110 0000000	31	219	222	0
20	00001111 11111111 10011110 0000000	15	255	158	0
21	00000111 11111111 00011110 0000000	7	255	30	0
22	00000000 10101000 00011110 0000000	0	172	30	0
23	00000000 00000000 00011110 0000000	0	0	30	0
24	00000000 00000000 00011110 0000000	0	0	30	0
25	00000000 00000000 00011110 0000000	0	0	30	0
26	00000000 00000000 00111110 0000000	0	0	62	0
27	00000000 00000000 00111100 0000000	0	0	60	0
28	00000000 00000000 01111100 0000000	0	0	124	0
29	00000000 00000001 11111000 0000000	0	1	248	0
30	00000001 11111111 11110000 0000000	1	255	240	0
31	00000011 11111111 11100000 0000000	3	255	224	0
32	00000001 11111111 10000000 0000000	1	255	128	0

Figure 2.15 Portrait character sample.

In PCL commands, the number one = 1; the lowercase letter "el" = l; the number zero = Ø; and the uppercase letter "oh" = O.

Dot Row	Bit Map	Decimal Equivalent			
01	01000000 00000000 00000000 00000000	64	0	0	0
02	11100000 00000000 00000000 00000000	224	0	0	0
03	11100000 00000000 00000000 00000000	224	0	0	0
04	11100000 00000000 00000000 00000000	224	0	0	0
05	11111111 11111111 11111111 11000000	255	255	255	192
06	11111111 11111111 11111111 11110000	255	255	255	240
07	11111111 11111111 11111111 11111000	255	255	255	248
08	01111111 11111111 11111111 11111100	127	255	255	252
09	00001111 10000111 11000000 01111110	15	135	192	126
10	00011110 00000001 11100000 00011110	30	1	224	30
11	00111000 00000000 11110000 00001111	56	0	240	15
12	01111000 00000000 01111000 00001111	120	0	120	15
13	01110000 00000000 00111000 00000111	112	0	56	7
14	11110000 00000000 00111000 00000111	240	0	56	7
15	11100000 00000000 00011100 00000111	224	0	28	7
16	11110000 00000000 00111000 00000111	240	0	56	7
17	11100000 00000000 00011100 00000111	224	0	28	7
18	11110000 00000000 00111000 00000111	240	0	56	7
19	11110000 00000000 00111100 00000111	240	0	60	7
20	01110000 00000000 00111000 00000111	112	0	56	7
21	01111000 00000000 01111000 00000010	120	0	120	2
22	01111100 00000000 11111000 00000000	124	0	248	0
23	00111111 00000011 11110000 00000000	63	3	240	0
24	00011111 11111111 11100000 00000000	31	255	224	0
25	00011111 11111111 11000000 00000000	31	255	192	0
26	00000111 11111111 10000000 00000000	7	255	128	0
27	00000001 11111100 00000000 00000000	1	252	0	0

Figure 2.16 Landscape character sample.

^{E}c*c1Ø3E where 103 is the ASCII value for "g"
^{E}c(144W character descriptor and data

The character descriptor is shown in Table 2.4, and the character data are shown in Figure 2.15.

In PCL commands, the number one = 1; the lowercase letter "el" = l; the number zero = Ø; and the uppercase letter "oh" = O.

Table 2.4 Sample character descriptor.

Field	Value	Description
Format	4	
Continuation	0	
Descriptor Size	14	
Class	1	
Orientation	0	Portrait
Reserved	0	
Left Offset	2	
Top Offset	22	
Character Width	27	
Character Height	32	
Delta X	120	30 dots

Macros

Macros are collections of individual printer commands that are frequently performed together. Rather than transmit the entire series of commands each time they are used, you can store them as a macro in the printer's memory and execute them as a set with a single command. This can save a great deal of time. PCL uses a series of commands to control the downloading, storing, naming, and execution of macros, as described below.

Defining a Macro

To begin the definition of a macro, you must first establish an ID number using the Macro ID command. You must then indicate the beginning of the macro definition by issuing the start macro definition command:

^{E}c&f3Y sets macro ID to 3
^{E}c&fØX starts macro definition

These commands can be combined into a single command as follows:

In PCL commands, the number one = 1; the lowercase letter "el" = l; the number zero = Ø; and the uppercase letter "oh" = O.

```
Ec&f3y0X
```

You then transmit the commands and data to be contained in the macro and terminate the definition mode with the command:

```
Ec&f1X
```

Running the Macro

There are three methods of running a macro: execution, calling, and overlaying. When you execute a macro, it alters the setting of the Current Defaults, just as if the commands were individually sent. When you call a macro, the macro commands are executed starting with the Current Default Environment. The Current Default Environment then resets to its values prior to running the macro. When you overlay a macro, it is run as the final task before printing each page. The overlay process stores the values of the Current Default Environment in memory, then restores the User Default Environment before starting. After finishing, the overlay process resets the values of the Current Default Environment to its values prior to starting the overlay.

To execute the current macro, use the command:

```
Ec&f2X
```

To call it, use the command:

```
Ec&f3X
```

And to enable it for overlay, use the command:

```
Ec&f4X
```

Since the overlay process is continuous (once for each page), you must explicitly turn it off with the command:

```
Ec&f5X
```

Deleting a Macro

You can delete macros one at a time, by type, or all at once. To delete the current macro, use the command:

```
Ec&f8X
```

To delete all temporary macros (i.e., macros that have been given the designation *temporary* so that they can be deleted and overwritten), use the command:

```
Ec&f7X
```

To delete all macros, use the command:

```
Ec&f6X
```

You can change the status of a macro to *permanent* (which prevents them from being deleted or overwritten) by using the command:

```
Ec&f10X
```

You can return it to the default temporary status with the command:

```
Ec&f9X
```

To set up a macro to create a one-inch by six-inch shaded box at the current position, assign it the ID #4, and execute it, enter and run the following BASIC program:

```
100 LPRINT CHR$(27);"&f4Y"      Specifies the ID #
200 LPRINT CHR$(27);"&f0X"      Starts macro definition
300 LPRINT CHR$(27);"*c300A"    Sets horizontal size
```

In PCL commands, the number one = 1; the lowercase letter "el" = l; the number zero = 0; and the uppercase letter "oh" = O.

```
400 LPRINT CHR$(27);"*c1800B"   Sets vertical size
500 LPRINT CHR$(27);"*c25G"     Selects shading percentage
600 LPRINT CHR$(27);"*c2P"      Starts drawing with shading
700 LPRINT CHR$(27);"&f1X"      Stops macro definition
800 LPRINT CHR$(27);"&f2X"      Executes macro
```

The cursor position is not considered to be part of the Current Default Environment and is not restored after a macro is called. If you want to return the cursor to the starting position after calling a macro, you must store the coordinates of the current cursor position using the Push command, and restore the cursor to that position at the end of the macro using the Pop command. In other words, the first macro command should be the Push command (^{E}c&f0S) and the last command should be the Pop command (^{E}c&f1S).

You can nest two layers of macro by having one macro call or execute another as part of its command file. Be sure that both macros are properly loaded and identified prior to running the calling macro. You cannot run a macro overlay command from within a macro.

You also cannot use any font management commands in a macro. For example, you can't change the status of a font from temporary to permanent from within a macro. You can store up to 32 macros in a LaserJet Series II printer at one time.

Patience Is the PCL Programmer's Greatest Asset

At this point, you know all the basic rules for writing even the most complex PCL printer language command strings. But regardless of your intended use for PCL and the complexity of the strings you write, precision is the name of the game. A single uppercase letter entered in lowercase form or vice versa will cause the command to be ignored by the printer. And neither DOS nor your LaserJet will give you any clues as to why. Worse, once you've tried to debug a lengthy PCL command string a couple of times, your chances of picking up the error diminish considerably. One of our great strengths, the ability to recognize patterns, is also our greatest weak-

In PCL commands, the number one = 1; the lowercase letter "el" = l; the number zero = 0; and the uppercase letter "oh" = O.

ness when it comes to programming. The solution? If you can't make a command work on the first or second try, have someone read you the code as you type it into the computer. Then read it back to verify that it's correct. Go slow, and the printer will be at your beck and call.

III SOFTWARE NOTES AND SUGGESTIONS

Lotus 1-2-3 Releases 1A, 2.0, and 2.01

Lotus Development Corp.
55 Cambridge Parkway
Cambridge, MA 02142

Technical Support: (617) 253-9150
Hours: (M–F) 8:30A.M. – 8:00 P.M. EST

Highlights

- Overview
- Setup
  - Installation
  - Interface
  - Default Setup Strings
- Common Setup Strings
  - Setting Tighter Letter Spacing to Simulate a Smaller Font
  - Changing the Line Spacing to Increase the Number of Lines
- Per Inch
- Using Fonts

Overview

Lotus 1-2-3 offers little in the way of support for the LaserJet, other than fixed spacing (see below). If you want to print in condensed or bold, you can enter the appropriate command string (see below) through the /**P**rint **P**rinter **O**ptions **S**etup command (**/PPOS**). You cannot, however, select print attributes from a Lotus menu. A number of third-party RAM resident software programs are currently available for that task, and are listed in the *HP LaserJet Printer Family Software and Hardware Solutions Guide*, available from Hewlett-Packard.

Setup

Installation

Follow the 1-2-3 installation instructions, in the "Getting Started" booklet included with the program. When you are asked what kind of text printer you have, you will have to choose between an unlisted and a LaserJet printer. This is not as obvious as it seems. If you're using Release 2.0, HP recommends that you select *Unlisted*, rather than LaserJet or LaserJet PLUS. The reason is that the Release 2.0 driver for the LaserJet automatically issues an escape code, which can confuse the printer when combined with your own PCL code.

> **Note:** If you do select Unlisted for your text printer, you will not find a counterpart when you select a graphics printer, so you will have to select HP LaserJet/LaserJet PLUS.

Interface

If you select Unlisted Printer or HP LaserJet/LaserJet PLUS, 1-2-3 will automatically set your interface for parallel port LPT1:. If your LaserJet is set up for serial operation, or for another parallel port, you can change the interface after you leave the install program and enter 1-2-3. To do so, start 1-2-3, then execute the following commands:

1. /**W**orksheet **G**lobal **D**efault **P**rinter
2. Select **I**nterface from the options shown in the menu panel.
3. The menu panel will display 1 2 3 4 5 6 7 8 with the highlight over the 1. Each time you press the right cursor key, the highlight will move one digit to the right. Use the left cursor key to move one digit to the left. The numbers correspond to the following interface settings.

1 = parallel 1 (LPT1:)

2 = serial 1 (COM1:)

3 = parallel 2 (LPT1:)

4 = serial 1 (COM2:)

5 = DOS Device LPT1:

6 = DOS Device LPT2:

7 = DOS Device LPT3:

8 = DOS Device LPT4:

When the highlight is over the desired interface setting, press **<RETURN>**, and the printer default menu will reappear. Select **Q**uit and the default menu will be displayed.

4. Select **U**pdate, and 1-2-3 will store your change and use the interface you selected whenever the program is run.

Default Setup Strings

When you leave the install program, Lotus will use the default font in your printer. If you want 1-2-3 to use another font, you can do so by starting 1-2-3 and typing the following commands:

1. /**W**orksheet **G**lobal **D**efault **P**rinter
2. Select **S**etup
3. The menu panel will display:

   ```
   Default Setup String:
   ```

4. Enter the desired string (choose from the tables below) and press **<RETURN>**. For example, if you always want-

ed your LaserJet to print in compressed print (16.66 characters per inch), you would enter the following string:

```
\027E\027(s16.66H
```

Note 1: This string assumes that you either have a LaserJet Series II, which has a built-in compressed font, or a cartridge that contains a 16.66-character-per-inch typeface. The following cartridges have 16.66 fonts: A,B,C,F,G,H,J,L,U,V, X,Y, and Z. Soft fonts DA and EA also have 16.66 fixed-spaced fonts.

Note 2: Be very careful to enter the string exactly as it appears in this book or your HP manual. Upper- and lowercase is critical, as is spacing. Be sure to distinguish one's and lowercase "el's", as well as uppercase "oh's" and zeroes "zero."

5. The menu will return to the printer default options. Select **Q**uit and the default options menu will appear.
6. Select **U**pdate and the worksheet will be ready for data entry. Every worksheet will now default to the printer setup string you entered through this procedure. You can still change an individual worksheet by using the **/PPOS** command and entering whatever string you need to accomplish your printing task. A list of commonly used setup strings is provided below.

Common Setup Strings

The following setup strings cover most general printing requirements. To print in 12 pitch, you must have a cartridge with 12 pitch fonts. Even if you don't have a 12 pitch font, you can simulate it by substituting **\027&k10H** for the **\027(s0p12H** that is shown in the 12 CPI setup strings below, which will print a 10 pitch font with 12 pitch spacing. Depending on the font, the results may be aesthetically acceptable.

All of the 16.16 pitch setup strings below require a font cartridge with condensed typefaces, or a printer with built-in condensed fonts (LaserJet Series II or LaserJet 2000).

Note: To print more than 100 lines per page, you must select the unformatted option **\PPOOU** each time before printing. This bypasses 1-2-3's built-in page length maximum of 100 lines per page.

Orientation: Portrait
Paper Size: Letter (8 1/2 by 11)
Paper Feed: Tray
 # Lines Per Page: 60

Pitch		*Setup String*	*Right Margin*
10	CPI	`\027E`	80
12	CPI	`\027(s0p12H`	96
16.66	CPI	`\027&k2S`	132

Orientation: Portrait
Paper Size: Letter (8 1/2 by 11)
Paper Feed: Tray
 # Lines Per Page: 66

Pitch		*Setup String*	*Right Margin*
10	CPI	`\027&l7.27C`	80
12	CPI	`\027&l7.27C\027(s0p12H`	96
16.66	CPI	`\027&l7.27C\027&k2S`	132

Orientation: Portrait
Paper Size: Letter (8 1/2 by 11)
Paper Feed: Tray
 # Lines Per Page: 89

Pitch		*Setup String*	*Right Margin*
10	CPI	\027&l5.39C	80
12	CPI	\027&l5.39C\027(s0p12H	96
16.66	CPI	\027&l5.39C\027&k2S	132

Orientation: Portrait
Paper Size: Legal (8 1/2 by 14)
Paper Feed: Tray
 # Lines Per Page: 78

Pitch		*Setup String*	*Right Margin*
10	CPI	\027E	80
12	CPI	\027(s0p12H	96
16.66	CPI	\027&k2S	132

Orientation: Portrait
Paper Size: Legal (8 1/2 by 14)
Paper Feed: Tray
 # Lines Per Page: 104 (Note: Current versions of 1-2-3 only support a maximum of 100 lines per page.)

Pitch		*Setup String*	*Right Margin*
10	CPI	\027&l8D	80
12	CPI	\027&l8D\027(s0p12H	96
16.66	CPI	\027&l8D\027&k2S	132

In PCL commands, the number one = 1; the lowercase letter "el" = l; the number zero = 0; and the uppercase letter "oh" = O.

Orientation: Portrait
Paper Size: Legal (8 1/2 by 14)
Paper Feed: Tray
 # Lines Per Page: 150

Pitch		*Setup String*	*Right Margin*
16.66	CPI	`\027&l4.16C\027&k2S`	132

Orientation: Portrait
Paper Size: Legal (8 1/2 by 14)
Paper Feed: Manual
 # Lines Per Page: 78

Pitch		*Setup String*	*Right Margin*
10	CPI	`\027&l84p2H`	80
12	CPI	`\027&l84p2H\027(0p12H`	96
16.66	CPI	`\027&l84p2H\027&k2S`	132

Orientation: Portrait
Paper Size: Legal (8 1/2 by 14)
Paper Feed: Manual
 # Lines Per Page: 104

Pitch		*Setup String*	*Right Margin*
10	CPI	`\027&l84p2h8D`	80
12	CPI	`\027&l84p2h8D\027(s0p12H`	96
16.66	CPI	`\027&l84p2h8D\027&k2S`	132

Orientation: Portrait
Paper Size: Legal (8 1/2 by 14)
Paper Feed: Manual
 # Lines Per Page: 150

Pitch		*Setup String*	*Right Margin*
16.66	CPI	`\027&l84p2h4.16C\027&k2S`	132

In PCL commands, the number one = 1; the lowercase letter "el" = l; the number zero = Ø; and the uppercase letter "oh" = O.

Orientation: Landscape
Paper Size: Letter (8 1/2 by 11)
Paper Feed: Tray
 # Lines Per Page: 45

Pitch		*Setup String*	*Right Margin*
10	CPI	\027&l1O	106
12	CPI	\027&l1O\027(s0p12H	127
16.66	CPI	\027&l1O\027&k2S	176

Orientation: Landscape
Paper Size: Letter (8 1/2 by 11)
Paper Feed: Tray
 # Lines Per Page: 66

Pitch		*Setup String*	*Right Margin*
10	CPI	\027&l1o5.45C	106
12	CPI	\027&l1o5.45C\027(s0p12H	127
16.66	CPI	\027&l1o5.45C\027&k2S	176

Orientation: Landscape
Paper Size: Legal (8 1/2 by 14)
Paper Feed: Tray
 # Lines Per Page: 45

Pitch		*Setup String*	*Right Margin*
10	CPI	\027&l1O	136
12	CPI	\027&l1O\027(s0p12H	163
16.66	CPI	\027&l1O\027&k2S	226
17.75	CPI	\027&l1O\027&k2s6.75H	240

In PCL commands, the number one = 1; the lowercase letter "el" = l; the number zero = 0; and the uppercase letter "oh" = O.

Orientation: Landscape
Paper Size: Legal (8 1/2 by 14)
Paper Feed: Tray
 # Lines Per Page: 66

Pitch		*Setup String*	*Right Margin*
10	CPI	`\027&l1o5.45C`	136
12	CPI	`\027&l1o5.45C\027(s0p12H`	163
16.66	CPI	`\027&l1o5.45C\027&k2S`	226
17.75	CPI	`\027&l1o5.45C\027&k2s6.75H`	240

Orientation: Landscape
Paper Size: Legal (8 1/2 by 14)
Paper Feed: Manual
 # Lines Per Page: 45

Pitch		*Setup String*	*Right Margin*
10	CPI	`\027&l84p2h1O`	136
12	CPI	`\027&l84p2h1O\027(s0p12H`	163
16.66	CPI	`\027&l84p2h1O\027&k2S`	226
17.75	CPI	`\027&l84p2h1O\027&k2s6.75H`	240

Orientation: Landscape
Paper Size: Legal (8 1/2 by 14)
Paper Feed: Manual
 # Lines Per Page: 66

Pitch		*Setup String*	*Right Margin*
10	CPI	`\027&l84p2h5.45C`	136
12	CPI	`\027&l84p2h5.45C\027(s0p12H`	163
16.66	CPI	`\027&l84p2h5.45C\027&k2S`	226
17.75	CPI	`\027&l84p2h5.45C\027&k2s6.75H`	240

In PCL commands, the number one = `1`; the lowercase letter "el" = `l`; the number zero = `0`; and the uppercase letter "oh" = `O`.

Setting Tighter Letter Spacing to Simulate a Smaller Font

In the above examples, several compressed fonts have a spacing of 17.75 characters per inch. In fact, the characters are really designed to be 16.66 CPI, but have been squeezed closer together by altering what is called the Horizontal Motion Index (HMI), which defines the horizontal space allocated to each letter. (See Section II for more information about HMI and the structure of PCL command strings.)

Changing the Line Spacing to Increase the Number of Lines Per Inch

If you wish to print a number of lines other than those specified, you can change the Vertical Motion Index (VMI), which controls the spacing between lines. In the above Landscape setup strings, the VMI is a number followed by an uppercase C. You can change the line spacing to a greater or smaller value by specifying a different VMI. The VMI value is determined according to the following formula:

$$\text{VMI} = \frac{7.5}{\#\ \text{lines}} \times 48$$

In the above Landscape examples, the VMI is calculated as

$$\frac{7.5}{66} \times 48$$

which equals 5.45. If you do change the VMI, be sure to change the page length in 1-2-3 to correspond to the number of lines you selected. This is done with the **/PPOP** command.

If the setup string does not explicitly declare VMI, as in

```
\027&l84p2h1O
```

you will have to insert a value in the proper place according to the rules laid out in Section II.

Using Fonts

Releases 1A, 2.0, and 2.01 are only designed to manage the spacing of fixed-pitch fonts. You can use proportional fonts, but you will have to carry out one of three measures: (1) instruct the printer from DOS before loading 1-2-3 by means of a BASIC program (a number of them are included with the Laser-ToolKit disk and documentation); (2) execute a macro from within Lotus (again refer to the Laser-ToolKit—macros are included for the most popular HP cartridges, as well as for the 30-character-per-inch JetWare Lotica cartridge); or (3) use a third-party RAM resident font management program. Be aware, though, that regardless of how you effect the proportional spacing, what you see on the screen is *NOT* what you are likely to get out of the printer—column headings and other text probably won't line up on the first try, and you will have to keep experimenting by including leading spaces in front of the text to be set in proportional type (be prepared to waste a *lot* of paper).

At the time of this writing, the following cartridges and soft fonts contain fixed-pitch fonts:

Cartridge Fonts 92286:
  A, C, D, E, G, H, J, L, M, N, Q, R, Y
Cartridge Fonts 92290:
  S1 (LaserJet 2000 Series II and LaserJet 2500)
Soft Fonts 33411:
  DA, EA
Soft Fonts 33412:
  DA, EA

The following proportional fonts can be used if you follow the procedures described on page 128.

Cartridge Fonts 92286:
  B, F, K, P, T, U, V, W, X, Z
Cartridge Fonts 92290:
  S2
Soft Fonts 33411:
  AC, AD, AE, AF, RA, SA, TA, UA
Super Fonts 33412:
  AG

WORDPERFECT 4.2

WordPerfect Corporation
288 West Center St.
Orem, UT 84057

Technical Support: (800) 321-5906
Hours: (M–F) 7:00 A.M. – 6:00 P.M. MST
(Sat) 8:00A.M. – 12:00 P.M. MST

Highlights

- Overview
- Installing Your LaserJet Printer with WordPerfect
- Adding a LaserJet to an Existing Printer Configuration
- Starting from Scratch
- Changing Printers
- Printing Out a Font List: WordPerfect 4.2
- PrHelp Printout
- Printer Tests
- Changing Fonts Within a Document
- Proportional Fonts
- Printing on Envelopes
- LaserJet Series II Envelope Tray
- Using Legal Size Paper
- Custom Printer Definitions
- Editing a Printer Definition

Overview

WordPerfect 4.2 supports more than 30 font cartridges and soft fonts. You can select from up to eight fonts per printer definition to create elegant pages. The LaserJet Series II can handle up to 16 fonts per page.

Printer definitions for the following cartridges and soft fonts are available on WordPerfect's printer disk. The definitions automatically assign the proper font specification PCL strings to the various WordPerfect font numbers. After properly installing the correct printer definition, you can select a particular font simply by specifying the font number via the Print Format menu, **<SHIFT><F8>**. (Note: you can create custom printer definitions for fonts not currently supported by the program. This is also explained later in this section.)

Font Source	*WordPerfect Printer Definition*	
Internal Fonts		
LaserJet	LaserJet Reg, +,500+ A:	Courier
LaserJet	LaserJet Reg, +,500+ A:	Courier
LaserJet	LaserJet Reg, +,500+ A:	Courier
Series II	HP LaserJet Series II	
Font Cartridges		
92286A	LaserJet Reg, +,500+ A:	Courier
92286B	LaserJet Reg, +,500+ B:	Tms Rmn1
92286C	LaserJet Reg, +,500+ C:	Intl1 Courier
92286D	LaserJet Reg, +,500+ D:	Prestige Elite
92286E	LaserJet Reg, +,500+ E:	Letter Gothic
92286F	LaserJet Reg, +,500+ F:	Tms Rmn2
92286G	LaserJet Reg, +,500+ G:	Legal Prestige Elite
92286H	LaserJet Reg, +,500+ H:	Legal Courier
92286J	LaserJet Reg, +,500+ J:	Math Prestige Elite
92286K	LaserJet Reg, +,500+ K:	Tms Math
92286L	LaserJet Reg, +,500+ L:	Courier P&L
92286M	LaserJet Reg, +,500+ M:	Prestige Elite P&L
92286N	LaserJet Reg, +,500+ N:	Letter Gothic P&L
92286P	LaserJet Reg, +,500+ P:	Tms Rmn P&L
92286Q	LaserJet Reg, +,500+ Q:	Courier, Letter Gothic
92286R	LaserJet Reg, +,500+ R:	Presentation
92286T	LaserJet Reg, +,500+ T:	Helv Tax
92286U	LaserJet Reg, +,500+ U:	Forms Portrait
92286W	LaserJet Reg, +,500+ W:	Bar Code
92286Y	LaserJet Reg, +,500+ Y:	PC Courier
92286Z	LaserJet Reg, +,500+ Z:	Helv/Tms Rmn
Soft Fonts		
33412AC (Portrait)	LaserJet+,500+ Soft AC:	Helv Portrait
	LaserJet+,500+ Soft AC:	Tms Rmn Portrait
33412AE (Portrait)	LaserJet+,500+ Soft AE:	Helv Portrait
	LaserJet+,500+ Soft AE:	Tms Rmn Portrait
33412DA (Portrait)	LaserJet+,500+ Soft DA:	Letter Gothic, Prestige Elite
33412EA (Portrait)	LaserJet+,500+ Soft EA:	Prestige Elite

Installing Your LaserJet Printer with WordPerfect

WordPerfect allows you to select printer definitions for up to six printers. If you had the hardware, you could conceivably have six different printers running off the program. Or, in the case of the LaserJet, you can set up the printer for eight different cartridges or soft fonts. Printer 1 is the definition that WordPerfect defaults to until you instruct it to use another definition. Other printers can be used for specific printing tasks.

For example, Printer 1 might be installed as a plain vanilla LaserJet Series II, Printer 2 might be assigned definitions for Cartridge G, Prestige Elite, while Printer 3 might be installed for the cartridge F, proportional Times Roman or Helvetica. Printer 1 would be used for normal everyday printing, while Printer 2 might be used for correspondence, and Printer 3, with its proportional spacing, might be called in for doing bulletins and special reports. We'll discuss switching printers later in this section.

Installation is very simple once you understand the not-so-obvious numbering system used to assign each printer a definition. WordPerfect supplies printer definitions (drivers) on separate diskettes with sequential numbers assigned to each definition. The number assigned to a particular definition will vary depending on which release of the printer definitions you are using. When you select a definition from the diskette to install on your system, it is copied to your WordPerfect directory or diskette and assigned a NEW definition number based on the order in which you installed it. For example, the printer definition for the HP LaserJet Series II might be number 99 on the WordPerfect Printer Disk, but will be number 4 on your system, if it was the fourth printer definition you installed.

In the following pages, we'll set up WordPerfect for three printer definitions: 1 = LaserJet Series II; 2 = Cartridge G; and 3 = Cartridge F, as in the above hypothetical configuration. The installation procedure described below assumes that you have not installed any printers before. The next section explains what to do when you are adding a LaserJet to a WordPerfect program that already has installed printer definitions.

WordPerfect Installation Procedure

To set up Printer 1 as a LaserJet Series II, internal fonts, use the following procedure.

1. Start WordPerfect
2. Press **<SHIFT> <F7>**
3. Select option **[4]**, Printer Control.
4. Choose option **[3]**, Select Printers.
   You will see the display shown in Figure 3.1.
   Notice the bottom-left corner of the screen, where it says Printer 1 Using Definition 1. In fact, at this point Printer 1 has no definition, and you must give it one. To do so, press the **<PgDn>** key. WordPerfect will display the message shown in Figure 3.2.
5. Insert the disk labeled Printer 1 into the A or B drive, then type in the letter of whichever drive you're using. WordPerfect will then display a numbered list of printers, arranged alphabetically. The specific numbers assigned to each definition will vary depending on which release of the definitions you are using.
6. Press **<PgDn>** twice and the list will continue. If you overshoot the part of the list containing your printer, press the **<PgUp>** key to cycle back to the previous screen. Type in **65** corresponding to the HP LaserJet Series II and press **<RETURN>**. Again, the specific number may vary on your system.
7. The screen will now prompt you to select a port. If your printer is set up for parallel operation, select option **0**, for LPT1: (or whatever parallel port you're using). If the printer is set up for serial operation, select whatever port the printer is connected to, then press **<RETURN>**. (In this case, we'll set up the printer for LPT1:—see Figure 3.3.)

```
Printer Definitions in C:\WP\WPRINTER.FIL









                                    PgDn for Additional Printer Definitions
                                    Exit when Done
Printer 1                           Cancel to Ignore Changes
Using Definition: 1                 Arrow Keys to Change Printer Number
```

Figure 3.1 WordPerfect 4.2 printer definition screen.

```
Can't Find Printer Files...

    Place a WordPerfect Printer Diskette
    in any floppy disk drive other than drive C:

     (If you don't have another floppy disk drive, you must
     install WordPerfect properly on your system before you
     can select printers.  See the "Getting Started" section
     of your WordPerfect manual for help with this.)

Press Drive Letter When Ready:
```

Figure 3.2 WordPerfect 4.2 printer disk message.

8. Next, WordPerfect will ask you to select the type of paper feed mechanism on your printer. You can select option **[1]**, Continuous, and the printer will work fine. HP recommends, however, that you select option **[3]**, Sheet Feeder, as it will facilitate envelope printing (see Figure 3.4).
9. WordPerfect will now request certain information about the Sheet Feeder. Select **[0]** for the first two options: Number of extra lines between pages, and Column position of left edge of paper. For the third option, Number of sheet feeder bins, enter the highest number available (7 in this case; see Figure 3.5).
10. Next, select the sheet feeder type. Enter **11** for HP LaserJet 500+, even if you have a LaserJet Series II (see Figure 3.6).
11. At this point, WordPerfect will return to the printer definition screen you encountered in the beginning of the process. The bottom-left corner of the screen now says `Printer 2, Using Definition 1.` Press **<PgDn>** again, and repeat the process, only in step 6 substitute the number for the G cartridge (number 99 in the example). When WordPerfect returns to the definition screen, repeat the process one more time, substituting the appropriate number for the F cartridge in step 6. The screen will appear as shown in Figure 3.7.

```
Printer Port
     0 - LPT 1    1 - LPT 2    2 - LPT 3
     4 - COM 1    5 - COM 2    6 - COM 3    7 - COM 4
     8 - Device or File Pathname
Selection: 0
```

***Figure 3.3** WordPerfect 4.2 printer port selection menu.*

```
Printer Port
     0 - LPT 1    1 - LPT 2    2 - LPT 3
     4 - COM 1    5 - COM 2    6 - COM 3    7 - COM 4
     8 - Device or File Pathname
Selection: 0

Type of Forms
    1 - Continuous
    2 - Hand Fed
    3 - Sheet Feeder
Selection: 3
```

***Figure 3.4** WordPerfect 4.2 form type selection menu.*

```
Sheet Feeder Information
     Number of Extra Lines Between Pages (12 LPI):  0
     Column Position of Left Edge of Paper (10 Pitch):  0
     Number of Sheet Feeder Bins (1-7):  7
```

Figure 3.5 WordPerfect 4.2 sheet feeder information menu.

```
Sheet Feeder Information
     Number of Extra Lines Between Pages (12 LPI):  0
     Column Position of Left Edge of Paper (10 Pitch):  0
     Number of Sheet Feeder Bins (1-7):  7

Sheet Feeder Type

    1 Apple LaserWriter                  2 BDT LetterMate I,II,III
    3 BDT MF-830 6 bin Laser Feeder      4 BDT MF-830 6 bin La (continued)
    5 BDT MF-850 3 bin Laser Feeder      6 BDT MF-850 3 bin La (continued)
    7 Brother HR-15/HR-25/HR-35          8 Canon A1
    9 Diablo Single/Dual/Envl           10 Epson LQ-1500 Single/Dual
   11 HP LaserJet 500+                  12 HP LaserJet 500+    (continued)
   13 IBM 5218 Dual Bin/Envl Feed       14 IBM Pageprinter 3812
   15 NEC 3515/5515/7715 Single/Dual    16 NEC 3550 Single/Dual
   17 Qume Single Bin                   18 Rutishauser Dual Bin
   19 Texas Instruments 2015            20 Xerox 2700 Laser
   21 Ziyad PaperJet 400                22 Ziyad PaperJet 400  (continued)

Selection: 11          (Use the PRINTER program to define a new sheet feeder)
```

Figure 3.6 WordPerfect 4.2 sheet feeder type selection menu.

Here's where things get tricky. The top of the screen lists your printer choices and the definition numbers that have been assigned to them as you selected them from the Printer Disk. The bottom of the screen indicates that you are ready to set up Printer 4. The top of the screen shows the printer definitions you've selected. Press the **<UP>** cursor key twice and the Printer number will change to 2. Notice that "Using definition" changes to 2, meaning that Printer 2 is set up with the number 2 definition corresponding to the G cartridge. Press the **<UP>** cursor again, and the lower-left screen will display `Printer 1, Using Definition 1`, indicating that it is configured with the number 1 printer definition corresponding to the LaserJet Series II. Press **<F7>** to exit the printer definition process and return to WordPerfect.

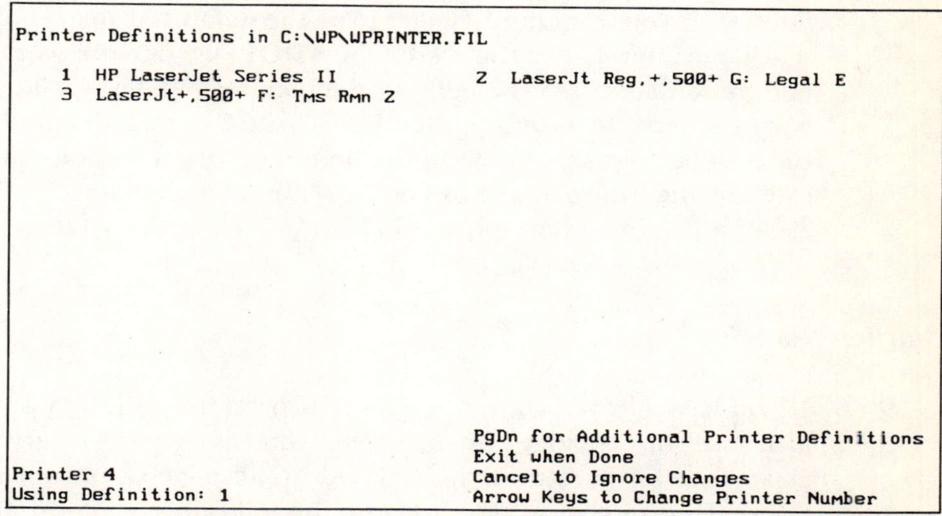

Figure 3.7 WordPerfect 4.2 printer definition screen after selecting printers.

If you ever need to display which printers you've set up, press **<SHIFT> <F7>**, then select option **[4]**. Next, select option **[2]**, and your printer setup file will be displayed.

The same process is used to specify any of the HP soft fonts that are explicitly supported by WordPerfect printer definitions. We'll discuss the process for setting up custom definitions for soft fonts that are not supported by WordPerfect later in this section.

Adding a LaserJet to an Existing Printer Configuration

If you wish to add a LaserJet to existing printer definitions, repeat the above procedure. The situation may get confusing if the LaserJet is, say, the third or fourth printer on your selected definition list. If you want the LaserJet to be the default (primary) printer, that is, Printer 1, use the **<UP>** or **<DOWN>** cursors so that the bottom-left corner of the definition screen says `Printer 1`. Disregard the current number after `Using Definition`, and enter the number corresponding to the definition of your choice, as indicated by the listing on the top of the screen. Do the same for Printer 2, 3, and so on. Then, press **<F7>** to exit from the screen.

Starting from Scratch

If you have already configured a set of printers, and then purchase a new set of cartridges or soft fonts, you may want to start with a clean slate (or have to if you've filled up all possible printer definitions). To do so, you'll have to erase the following printer definition files:

wprinter.fil

wpfont.fil

wpfeed.fil

These files will be located in the directory containing your WordPerfect program files. As soon as you define a printer, WordPerfect will create a new set of printer definition files.

Changing Printers

Once you've defined several printers, you can switch between them as you desire. Continuing with our example, Printer 1 corresponds to the LaserJet Series II. If you want to print a letter in Prestige Elite, which is Printer 2, carry out the following steps to make Printer 2 the current printer:

1. Press **<SHIFT> <F7>**
2. Select option **[4]**, Printer Control
3. Select option **[1]**, Select Print Options
4. Press **[1]** for Printer Number. Enter **2**, and press **<RETURN>**.
5. Press **<ESC>** or **<RETURN>** twice. The LaserJet will now be ready to print the fonts on the Prestige Elite, G cartridge

The next step in printing out is to indicate which fonts you wish to use at various points in the document. First, it will be helpful to print out a font list and font sample, as described below.

Printing out a Font List: WordPerfect

When you have several font cartridges defined, it is helpful to have a list of the numbers WordPerfect assigns to each font. You can do this by running a program called PRHELP.COM, which is located on your Learning Diskette. The output from PRHELP also summarizes the functions supported by each font.

Yet another type of font printout can be generated from within WordPerfect, with PRINTER.TST and PRINTER2.TST. Both files are included on your Learning Diskette. Whereas the PRHELP file lists the font assignments, the printer tests actually show you the various fonts, underline styles, and other capabilities. The following discussions explain how to use the various font printouts.

PRHELP Printout

1. Load the program. If you are using a floppy disk, and if the PRHELP.COM file is on a working diskette, type

   ```
   PRHELP
   ```

   from the prompt corresponding to your disk drive.

   If you have copied PRHELP.EXE to a directory on your hard disk, make that directory the current directory, then type

   ```
   PRHELP
   ```

2. The screen will display a list of printers, arranged alphabetically. Use the **<PgUp>** and **<PgDn>** keys to display the portion of the list containing the printer(s) you've selected, then use the cursor keys to position the highlighted bar over a specific printer. Press **<RETURN>**, and complete information about the printer definition will be displayed. Samples from the PRHELP file for each of the printers we've defined are shown in Figures 3.8(a) and (b). Note that the menu along the bottom of the screen gives you the opportunity to directly view the printer definition summaries by paging backward and forward through the list (**[2]** to move to the previous printer on the list, **[3]** to move to the next printer).

To make a hardcopy of the font definitions, use **<SHIFT>** **<PRTSC>**. Alternately, if you want to manipulate the output, use a screen grabbing program such as HotShot or HotShot Graphics. (All the figures in this section were created using HotShot and a LaserJet Series II.)

Printer Tests

The printer tests are printed out as you would any other WordPerfect file. The tests demonstrate the font and printing capability for whatever printer you have selected as the current printer.

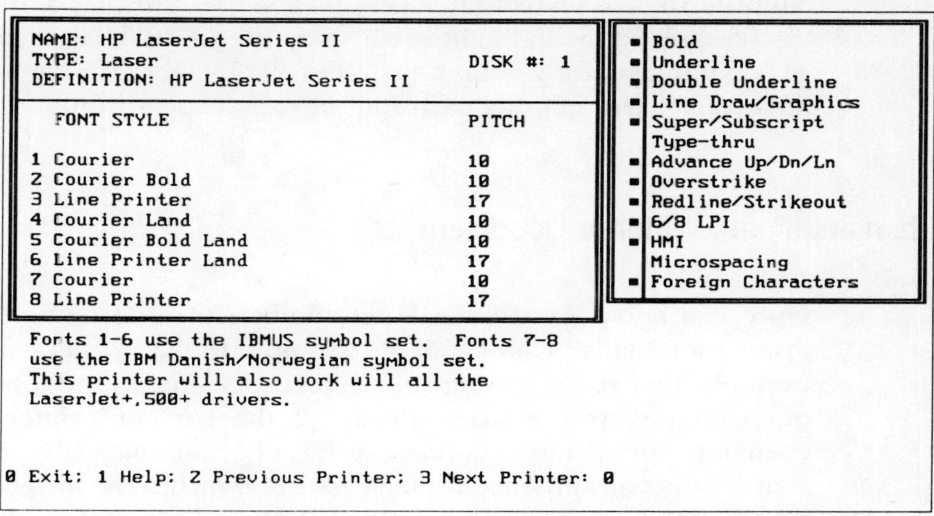

***Figure 3.8a** WordPerfect 4.2 font description from PRHELP file for LaserJet Series II.*

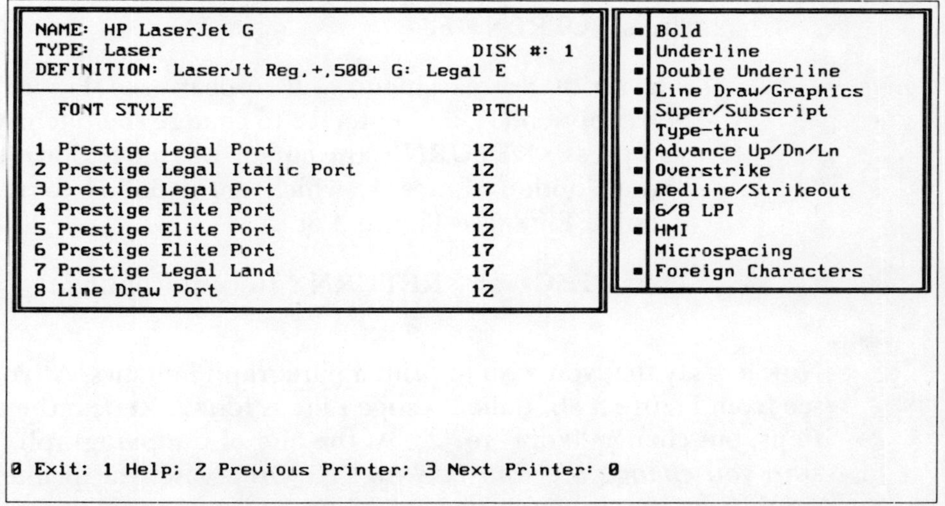

***Figure 3.8b** WordPerfect 4.2 font description from PRHELP file for G cartridge.*

To print the file PRINTER.TST, press **<F5>** to display a listing of the files, place the highlighted bar over PRINTER.TST, then press **4**. A multipage test will then print out. PRINTER2.TST generates an auxiliary test showing each font in various pitch configurations.

Changing Fonts Within a Document

Once you know WordPerfect's ID number for each font, you can insert font change commands in appropriate places. Let's say, for example, that you are using your G cartridge (i.e., in the context of our example, you've made Printer 2 the current printer). Just changing the Printer number does not automatically instruct WordPerfect to shift into 12-pitch spacing, which is the proper pitch for Prestige Elite. To print in regular Prestige Elite, you would need to do the following:

1. Make sure the cursor is in the upper-left corner of the document. This will format the entire document for normal Prestige printing, until you issue another font change command.

2. Press **<CTRL> <F8>**

3. The Print Format menu will appear (see Figure 3.9). Select option **[1]**, and enter **12** to change the pitch. When you press **<RETURN>**, the cursor will move down to the "Font" option. Enter **1**, which corresponds to regular Prestige Elite (see Figure 3.8b).

4. Press **<ESC>** or **<RETURN>** twice to continue.

Now lets say that you wish to print a paragraph in italics. As you can see from Figure 3.8b, Italic Prestige Elite is font 2. Repeat the above steps, but change "Font" to "2". At the end of the paragraph, *make sure you change the font back to "1."* Otherwise, the printer will continue to output text in the italic font. This same principle applies to all font cartridges and soft fonts.

```
Print Format

     1 - Pitch                    10
         Font                     1

     2 - Lines per Inch           6

   Right Justification            Off
     3 - Turn off
     4 - Turn on

   Underline Style                5
     5 - Non-continuous Single
     6 - Non-continuous Double
     7 - Continuous Single
     8 - Continuous Double

     9 - Sheet Feeder Bin Number  1

     A - Insert Printer Command

     B - Line Numbering           Off

Selection: 0
```

Figure 3.9 WordPerfect 4.2 print format menu.

Tracing a Runaway Font

If your document has printed out in wall-to-wall italics, or sideways in Landscape mode, you need to locate the font change starting the runaway font and either delete it or add a subsequent font change to restore the printer to its regular font after the text that you really wish to be printed in the alternate font. Use the Search feature to speed up the process:

1. Press **<F2>**
2. Press **<CTRL> <F8>**
3. Select option **[1]**, Font, then press **<ESC>**. The cursor will stop at the first font change command it finds. Use the reveal codes function to find the exact location of the font for deletion. If you want to contain the font change, move the cursor to the end of the text that you wish to appear in the selected font, then issue a command to restore the font to the regular style.

Automating Font Commands

You can use WordPerfect's macro capabilities to write simple macros that initiate font commands. **<ALT><I>**, for example, might change the font to the number corresponding to italics. **<ALT><R>** might issue a command that sets the printer for the regular font. These will enable you to quickly turn italics on and off at selected places in the document. See the FONT.MAC macro in Section I. It is a useful font change macro for WordPerfect that automatically changes the font back to the previous font selection after a block of text.

Proportional Fonts

With fixed-pitch fonts, you indicate 10, 12, or 17 pitch after calling up the Print Format menu (**<CTRL><F8>**). (A pitch of 17 is for compressed or line printer fonts, which are actually 16.66 characters per inch.) With proportionally spaced fonts (e.g., Times Roman and Helvetica) you must use the pitch shown in the PRHELP program. All proportional fonts require a pitch specification that includes an asterisk, such as 10*, 13*, and so on. If you do not include the asterisk, centering, tabs, margins, and right justification will not be correct.

Printing on Envelopes

You can either print envelopes through the manual feed of your LaserJet, or with the envelope tray of the Series II.

Manual

1. Make sure you have a cartridge that supports a Landscape font. The LaserJet Series II and LaserJet 2000 have built-in Landscape printing capabilities.
2. Place or copy the address on a separate page at the end of the document.

3. Use the settings in Table 3.1 to format an address for the left-aligned manual feed system on the LaserJet, LaserJet PLUS, and LaserJet 500, and use the settings in Table 3.2 for the center-aligned manual feed system of the LaserJet Series II.

Table 3.1 Left-aligned manual feed system

Setting	*MONARC*	*COM-10*	*DL*	*C5*
Top Margin	46	50	50	62
Left Margin	45	50	50	50
Right Margin	70	90	80	85
Font Change	Enter desired Landscape font.			
Bin Number *	3	3	3	3

Table 3.2 Center-aligned manual feed system

Setting	*MONARC*	*COM-10*	*DL*	*C5*
Top Margin	20	24	24	36
Left Margin	30	35	35	35
Right Margin	70	90	80	85
Bin Number*	4	5	6	7

*Bin number is changed through the Print Format menu **<CTRL> <F8>**

Monarc = 3 7/8 × 7 1/2
Commercial 10 = 4 1/8 × 9 1/2
DL = 110 mm × 220 mm
C5 = 162mm × 229 mm

4. Press **<SHIFT> <F7>** and select the page print option **[2]**. The LaserJet will prompt you to insert an envelope.

LaserJet Series II Envelope Tray

Creating a Printer Definition

To use the optional LaserJet Series II tray with WordPerfect you will need to create a new sheet feeder definition. This is done with the PRINTER.EXE program supplied on your Printer 2 diskette. Use the following procedure:

1. Load the program. If the PRINTER.EXE file is on a working floppy diskette, type

   `PRINTER`

   from the prompt corresponding to your disk drive.

   If you have copied PRINTER.EXE to a directory on your hard disk, make that directory the current directory, then type

   `PRINTER`

2. From the menu, select option **[5]**, "Sheet Feeder Definitions."
3. Press **[A]** Create. Press **Y** when asked if there are more than three bins.
4. Select **[11]** from the list and press **<RETURN>**
5. A screen will be displayed with eight options (see Figure 3.10).

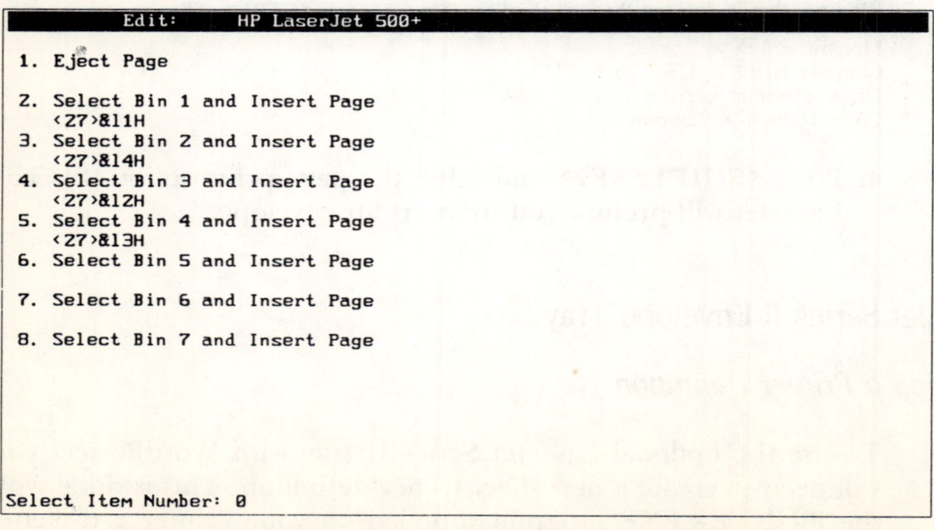

Figure 3.10 WordPerfect 4.2 printer definition editor.

Type **1**, and the cursor will move underneath option **[2]**. Fill in the line, as shown in Figure 3.11. When you finish, use the cursor to move down to the next line. Fill in the code as shown in Figure 3.11. Continue filling in each line, being careful to distinguish between lowercase Ls and ones, and zeroes and uppercase ohs. When you finish with the eighth line, press **<RETURN>**. Then press **[E]** to exit to the printer menu. Press **[0]** to return to the DOS prompt.

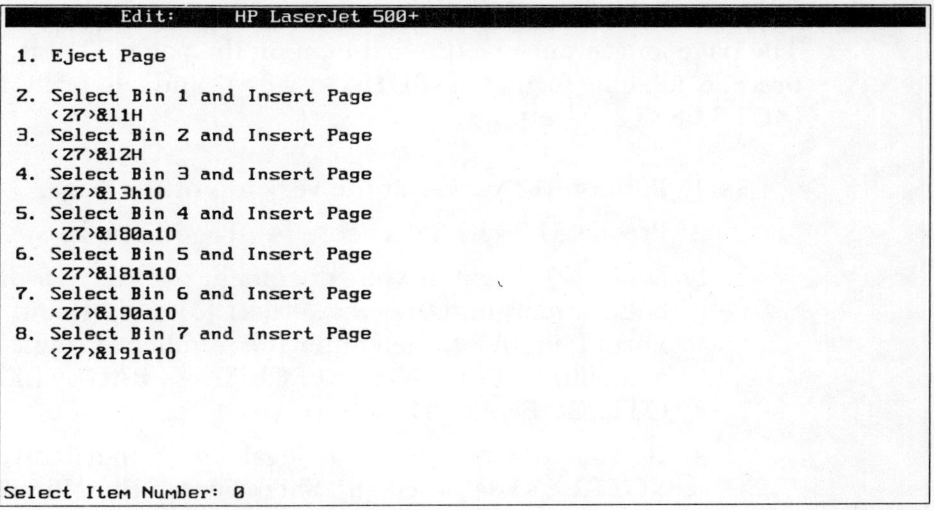

Figure 3.11 WordPerfect 4.2 printer definitions for creating envelope tray definition, LaserJet Series II.

Using the Tray

1. Insert up to 15 envelopes in the envelope tray and replace the cover.
2. Insert the tray firmly into the printer.
3. Set the envelope size using the control panel. Reset the printer.
4. Open the rear door of the printer.
5. Format the addresses using the values in Table 3.2. **VERY IMPORTANT!!**: You *must* set the format commands in the

order presented in Table 3.2. If you are typing a list of addresses, separate each one with a hard page (**<CTRL><RETURN>**).

6. Press **<SHIFT><F7>**, and select option **[1]**, Full Text, to print all the addresses.

Using Legal-Sized Paper

The page length must be the first item on the page. That is, it must precede all line format, (**<SHIFT><F8>**), and all print format, (**<CTRL><F8>**), settings.

1. Position the cursor at the very top of the page.
2. Press **<ALT><F8>**, choose **[4]**, Page Length.
3. Select **[2]**, Legal, if your document is to have a one-inch bottom margin. Otherwise, select **[3]**, Other, and specify Form Length 84, then enter the number of single-spaced text lines. DO NOT SPECIFY A PAGE LENGTH OTHER THAN 84.
4. If you do not have a legal-size paper tray, press **<CTRL><F8>**, select **[9]**, Sheet Feeder Bin Number, and specify bin number 3. Use bin number 2 if you created the HP LaserJet Series II sheet feeder definition.

When you print your document, wait until the printer requests legal paper. Then insert your legal paper tray, or manually feed a sheet of legal paper.

Custom Printer Definitions

If you download soft fonts that do not have a WordPerfect-supplied printer definition, you can either control the font selection by inserting PCL commands directly into the text using the Printer Command function or you can create a custom printer definition. The former is easier for a single-font change, while the latter is more efficient if you use the same soft fonts often.

To create or change the printer definitions, you can either use the PRINTER program, as described above for the envelope tray, or purchase WordPerfect's HP Utility ($15; call WordPerfect at 800-321-4566 to place an order). The special utility facilitates the creation of soft font print definitions, and will handle the downloading chores for you.

When using one of the following HP soft font packages, it is often easier to select and modify one of the existing WordPerfect printer definitions, using either the WordPerfect HP Utility or the PRINTER program. The specific modifications are listed by soft font disk:

Font	
92286V	Use the LaserJet Reg, +,500+ U: Forms Portrait printer definition as a pattern. Change the printerinitialization to **<27>&l1T<27>&l1O<27>(8U**
33412AC Landscape	Use either the LaserJet+,500+ Soft AC: Helv P or Tms P definition as a pattern. Replace **<27>&l0O** with **<27>&l1O** in the "Shift Into Font" strings.
33412AD Portrait	Use either the LaserJet+,500+ Soft AC: Helv P or Tms P definition as a pattern. Change **<27>(0U to <27>(8U** in the "Shift Into Font" strings.
33412AD Landscape	Use either the LaserJet+,500+ Soft AC: Helv P or Tms P definition as a pattern. Change **<27>(0U** to **<27>(8U** in the "Shift Into Font" strings. Also, replace **<27>&l0O** with **<27>&l1O** in the "Shift Into Font" strings.
33412AE Landscape	Use either the LaserJet+,500+ Soft AE: Helv P or Tms P definition as a pattern. Replace **<27>&l0O** with **<27>&l10** in the "Shift Into Font" strings.
33412AF Landscape	Use either the LaserJet+,500+ Soft AF: Helv P or Tms P definition as a pattern. Change **<27>(0U** to **<27>(8U** in the "Shift Into Font" strings. Also, replace **<27>&l0O** with **<27>&l1O** in the "Shift Into Font" strings.
33412DA Landscape	Use the LaserJet+,500+ Soft DA: Letter Gothic, Prestige Elite definition as a pattern. Replace **<27>&l0O** with **<27)&l1O** in the "Shift Into Font" strings.
33412EA Landscape	Use the LaserJet+,500+ Soft EA: Prestige Elite definition as a pattern. Replace **<27>&l0O** with **<27)&l1O** into the "Shift Into Font" strings.
33412RA	Purchase WordPerfect's HP Utility program.
33412SA	Purchase WordPerfect's HP Utility program.
33412TA	Purchase WordPerfect's HP Utility program.
33412UA	Purchase WordPerfect's HP Utility program.

Editing a Printer Definition

The paragraphs that follow take you through an example of using WordPerfect's PRINTER program to create a WP printer definition.

In this example, we will create a new printer definition to support Hewlett-Packard's 33412AD TmsRmn/Helv soft fonts.

As indicated earlier, WordPerfect supports HP's 33412AC TmsRmn/Helv soft fonts (USASCII symbol set). By modifying this definition's Shift Into Font sequences, you can create a new definition that supports the 33412AD (Roman 8 symbol set) soft fonts. The procedure is as follows:

1. Install the LaserJet+,500+ Soft AC: Tms P printer definition according to the instructions for printer definition installation earlier in this section. You must install this definition so that it can be used as a pattern in creating the new definition.
2. Load WordPerfect's PRINTER program. For a hard disk, copy the PRINTER.EXE program from your WP Printer 2 disk in the subdirectory from which you run WordPerfect. Then type **PRINTER** and press **<RETURN>**.
   For floppy disks, place your working copy of WordPerfect in Drive A and your WP Printer 2 disk in Drive B. At the A> prompt, type **B: PRINTER** and press **<RETURN>**. A menu should appear.
3. Select **[3]**, Printer Definitions (Examine, Change), at the PRINTER program menu.
4. Press **[A]**, Create. WordPerfect will prompt you to enter a new printer name. Type **LaserJet +,500+II AD: Tms P** and press **<RETURN>**.
5. Next, you will be asked to specify the current printer to use as a pattern. Enter the number assigned to the LaserJet+,500+ Soft AC: Tms P definition and press **<RETURN>**. A menu will appear.
6. Select **[8]**, Selecting Fonts (Fonts 1–4). WordPerfect will then display the current escape sequences used to select fonts 1–4 (see Figure 3.12).

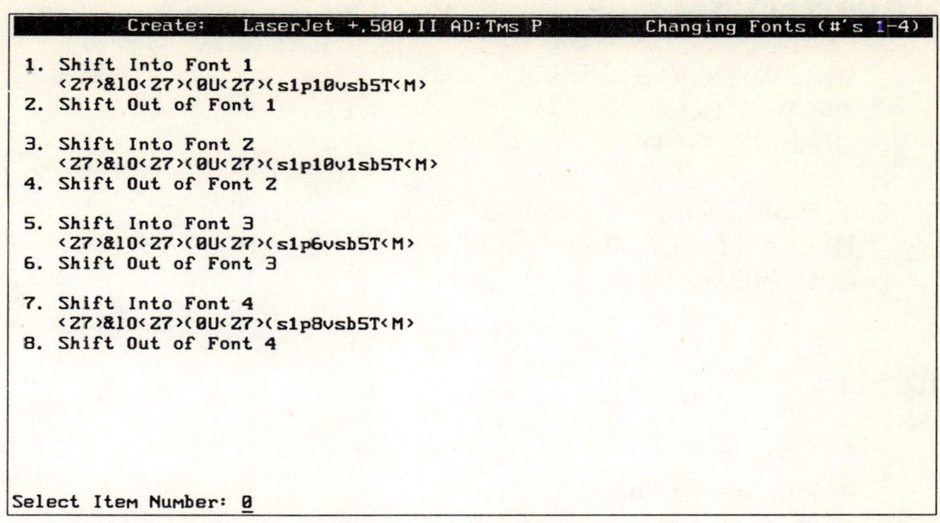

Figure 3.12 Wordperfect 4.2 customer printer definition.

7. The Custom Printer Definitions section of this document indicates that the **<27>(0U** portion of each "Shift Into Font" string must be changed to **<27>(8U** in order to support the 33412AD (Portrait) soft fonts. Thus, you would select item **[1]**, Shift Into Font 1, and change the **<27>(0U** to **<27>(8U** and press **<RETURN>**.
8. Repeat step seven for fonts 2–4.
9. Press **<RETURN>** at the "Select Item Number:" prompt to exit.
10. Select item **[9]**, Selecting Fonts (Fonts 5–8), to display the current escape sequences used to select fonts 5–8.
11. Repeat the same procedures as listed in steps 7–10 above, i.e., change the **<27>(0U** to **<27>(8U** in the "Shift Into Font" strings 5–8.
12. Press **<RETURN>** twice to exit the Printer Program.

This completes the creation of the LaserJet +,500+,II AD: Tms P printer definition. Simply load WordPerfect and assign this new definition to one of the six printers.

WordPerfect 5.0

WordPerfect Corporation
288 West Center St.
Orem, UT 84057

Technical Support: (800) 321-5906
Hours: (M–F) 7:00A.M. – 6:00 P.M. MST,
(Sat) 8:00A.M. – 12:00 P.M. MST

Highlights

- Overview
- Supported Fonts
- Installing your LaserJet Printer
- Printing on Envelopes
- Using Legal-Size Paper

Overview

WordPerfect 5.0 provides support for more than 30 font cartridges and soft font sets. The LaserJet Series II can handle up to 16 fonts per page. Printer definitions for the following cartridges and soft fonts are available on WordPerfect's printer disk. The definitions automatically assign the proper font specification PCL strings to the various WordPerfect font selections. After properly installing the correct printer definition, you can select a particular font simply by specifying the Base Font on the Font menu, **<CTRL> <F8>**, choosing option **[4]**. Highlight the desired font from the menu of available options, and press either **1** or **S** to select it. Once you've selected a Base Font, you can select variations by again pressing **<CTRL> <F8>** for the Font menu and selecting either the size or appearance options. As their names imply, size allows you to change the size of the type, while appearance covers such features as bold, underline, italic, outline, and so on.

You can specify any font as the Base Font, as long as it is available. Variations on the Base Font, such as bold, italics, or even a larger point size, can be specified from the font menu so long as the variation font is also available on the printer. If the variation is not available, the nearest available font will be used. You can easily determine which sizes and variations are available on your printer by printing the PRINTER.TST file. It contains samples of all font attributes and many of the common combinations, and will show you how they will appear with the fonts available on your printer.

Font Source	*WordPerfect Printer Definition*		
Internal Fonts			
LaserJet	LaserJet Reg, +,500+	A:	Courier
LaserJet	LaserJet Reg, +,500+	A:	Courier
LaserJet	LaserJet Reg, +,500+	A:	Courier
Series II	HP LaserJet Series II		
Font Cartridge			
92286A	LaserJet Reg, +,500+	A:	Courier
92286B	LaserJet Reg, +,500+	B:	Tms Rmn1
92286C	LaserJet Reg, +,500+	C:	Intl1 Courier
92286D	LaserJet Reg, +,500+	D:	Prestige Elite
92286E	LaserJet Reg, +,500+	E:	Letter Gothic
92286F	LaserJet Reg, +,500+	F:	Tms Rmn2
92286G	LaserJet Reg, +,500+	G:	Legal Prestige Elite
92286H	LaserJet Reg, +,500+	H:	Legal Courier
92286J	LaserJet Reg, +,500+	J:	Math Prestige Elite
92286K	LaserJet Reg, +,500+	K:	Tms Math
92286L	LaserJet Reg, +,500+	L:	Courier P&L
92286M	LaserJet Reg, +,500+	M:	Prestige Elite P&L
92286N	LaserJet Reg, +,500+	N:	Letter Gothic P&L
92286P	LaserJet Reg, +,500+	P:	Tms Rmn P&L
92286Q	LaserJet Reg, +,500+	Q:	Courier, Letter Gothic
92286R	LaserJet Reg, +,500+	R:	Presentation
92286T	LaserJet Reg, +,500+	T:	Helv Tax
92286U	LaserJet Reg, +,500+	U:	Forms Portrait
92286W	LaserJet Reg, +,500+	W:	Bar Code
92286Y	LaserJet Reg, +,500+	Y:	PC Courier
92286Z	LaserJet Reg, +,500+	Z:	Helv/Tms Rmn

Soft Font		
33412AC (Portrait)	LaserJet+,500+ Soft AC:	Helv Portrait
	LaserJet+,500+ Soft AC:	Tms Rmn Portrait
33412AE (Portrait)	LaserJet+,500+ Soft AE:	Helv Portrait
	LaserJet+,500+ Soft AE:	Tms Rmn Portrait
33412DA (Portrait)	LaserJet+,500+ Soft DA:	Letter Gothic, Prestige Elite
33412EA (Portrait)	LaserJet+,500+ Soft EA:	Prestige Elite

Installing Your Laserjet Printer with WordPerfect

WordPerfect 5.0 addresses the unique requirements of each printer by installing a printer definition file describing the specifications of the printer. These printer specifications are contained on one of the printer disks supplied with WordPerfect 5.0. WordPerfect 5.0 allows you to set up multiple printer definitions at the same time. You can select from among the specified printers by choosing the Selection option for the Print menu. With a sophisticated printer, such as an HP LaserJet, LaserJet PLUS, LaserJet 500 PLUS, or LaserJet Series II, you can have more than one logical configuration using different combinations of font cartridges and downloadable soft fonts. Each of these configurations can be thought of as a different *logical printer*. Each of these logical printers can be set up with its own printer definition file that describes the printer's features and tells WordPerfect 5.0 how to communicate with it and the various combinations of font cartridges and soft fonts. The number of fonts and cartridges that you can include in a given printer definition depends on the number of slots and the amount of memory available on your particular printer, and on whether you define the font or cartridge as being "always present" or "available to be loaded."

With LaserJet printers using a variety of cartridges and/or downloadable soft fonts for different print jobs, you have two strategies for setting up your printer definitions: You can set up one printer for all possible fonts and cartridges and instruct WordPerfect to notify you when to insert new cartridges, or you can set up separate logical printers, each with different cartridge and font configurations. The decision on which method to use will depend for the most part on the types of different documents you print and on how often you switch between fonts and font cartridges. If, for example, you use two distinctly different printer configurations for different types of documents, you may find it easier to set up two different logical printers, each with its own font and cartridge configuration. If you change fonts frequently, or if you have no distinct pattern of font usage, you may find it easier to load all your font and cartridge capabilities into one printer definition and select from among all the available fonts each time you want to change fonts. You will probably have to experiment with both techniques to determine which will work best for your situation.

Before you start to install a new printer definition, you will need to collect several pieces of information. You need to know the type of printer you are installing (LaserJet, LaserJet PLUS, or LaserJet Series II printer), the number of cartridge slots available on your printer, the total amount of user memory available on your printer, and the cartridges and soft fonts you plan to install. If you have not added any memory to your printer, you can accept the default memory configurations and do not need to know the actual amount of memory available.

To begin the installation process, place the Printer 1 disk in drive A: and bring up the Print Menu by pressing **<SHIFT><F7>**. Choose the Select Printer option by pressing **<S>**. You will be presented with a Select Printer screen that shows the printers that you have already installed; if this is your first printer installation, the screen will be blank (see Figure 3.13). Since you are adding a new printer, select **[A]**, Additional Printer. If you have copied the printer disks to the default directory, you will skip the following step, but most users will need to tell WordPerfect where to look for the printer files. If you are presented with the screen shown in Figure 3.14, you need to tell WordPerfect to look at the disk in the A: drive. Select option **[2]**, Other Disk, and enter **A** at the prompt. You will be shown a list of printers represented on the disk in Drive A: (see Figure 3.15). If your printer is not there, exchange the printer disk for the next in the series and repeat the above steps. When you have found your printer, select it by pointing to it with the highlighted cursor and choose option **[1]**, Select.

```
Print: Select Printer

* HP LaserJet Series II
  QMS PS JET+ (Postscript)

1 Select; 2 Additional Printers; 3 Edit; 4 Copy; 5 Delete; 6 Help: 1
```

Figure 3.13 WordPerfect 5.0 select printer screen

```
Select Printer: Additional Printers

Printer files not found

     Use the Other Disk option to specify a directory for the printer
     files.  Continue to use this option until you find the disk with the
     printer you want.

1 Select; 2 Other Disk; 3 Help; 4 List Printer Files; N Name Search: 1
```

Figure 3.14 WordPerfect 5.0 additional printer screen.

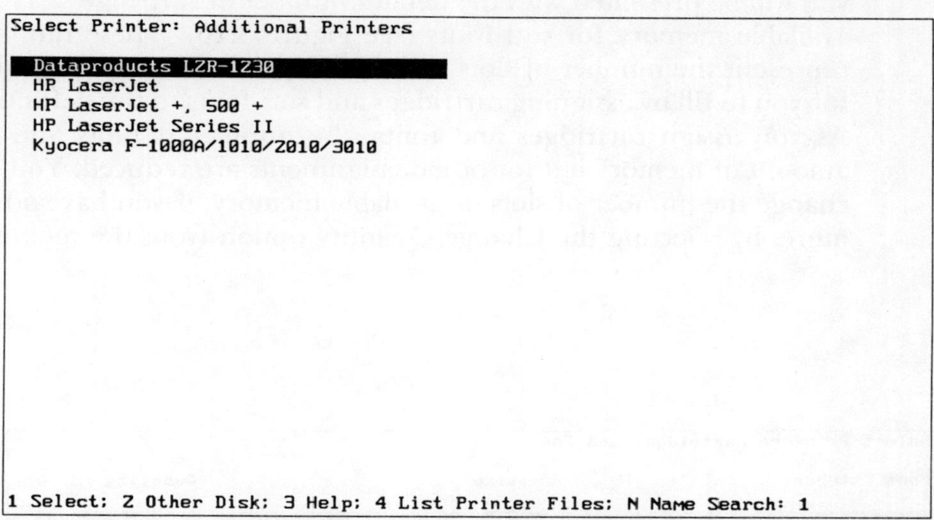

Figure 3.15 WordPerfect 5.0 printer disk listing.

The system will copy the necessary printer definition file to the WordPerfect directory, and then ask you to provide more specific information about your particular installation. You can edit the name that will appear on the Printer Selection Menu, if you choose, and can reassign the port to LPT2: or one of the serial ports if you need to. Simply select the option and enter the data or make the selection from the subsequent menus. You will have to specify the types of forms that are available. This will permit you to select different page sizes from the Format menu. If you do not specify that you have legal-size forms available on your printer, either as cartridge-fed sheets or manually fed sheets, you will not be able to specify legal paper from the Format menu. See below for more information on paper size specifications.

The most important part of setting up a printer definition is the specification of the cartridges and soft fonts available on the printer. If you are going to use downloadable soft fonts, you must also tell WordPerfect where the font files are located via the Printer Setting menu. This is done via option **[7]** on the menu. After defining the path for your soft fonts, you are ready to specify the individual fonts and cartridges for the printer definition. This is done via option **[5]**, Cartridges and Fonts. When you install a new printer definition, you will be presented with the default number of cartridge slots and available memory for soft fonts (see Figure 3.16). These numbers represent the number of slots and the amount of memory available for you to fill by assigning cartridges and soft fonts to the definition. As you assign cartridges and fonts, the number of slots and the amount of memory left for other assignments are reduced. You can change the number of slots or available memory, if you have added more, by selecting the Change Quantity option from the menu.

```
Select Printer: Cartridges and Fonts

Font Category                 Resource                      Quantity

Cartridge Fonts               Font Cartridge Slot               2
Soft Fonts                    Memory available for fonts     2000 K

1 Select Fonts: 2 Change Quantity: N Name search: 1
```

Figure 3.16 WordPerfect 5.0 slot/memory quanities

After setting the slot and memory quantities and specifying the location of soft fonts, you can select the cartridges and fonts to include in this particular printer definition. You do this by selecting either Cartridge Fonts or Soft Fonts by pointing at the option and then choosing option **[1]**, Select Fonts. You will be presented with a menu of the fonts and cartridges available for the printer you selected. You will also be given a number representing the number of cartridges or the amount of available RAM remaining to be assigned to cartridges or fonts (see Figures 3.17 and 3.18).

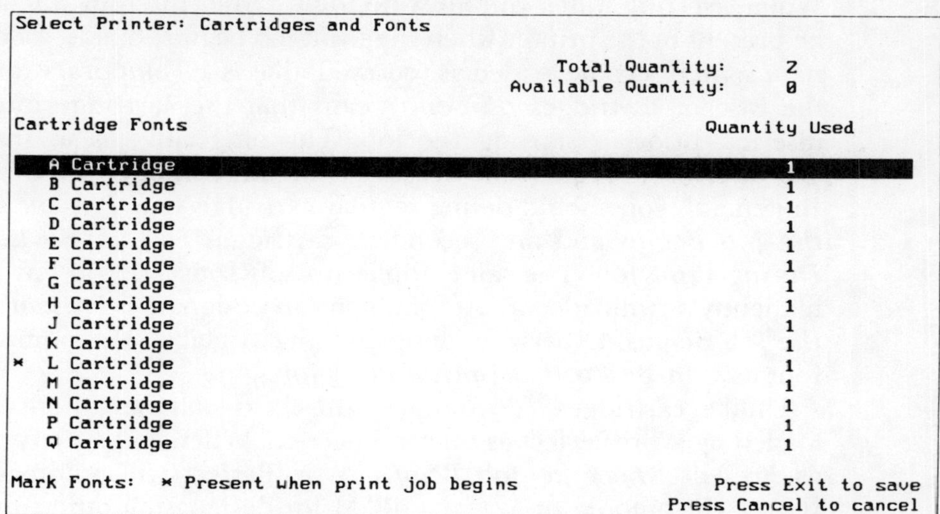

```
Select Printer: Cartridges and Fonts

                                          Total Quantity:      2
                                      Available Quantity:      0

Cartridge Fonts                                          Quantity Used

   A Cartridge                                                 1
   B Cartridge                                                 1
   C Cartridge                                                 1
   D Cartridge                                                 1
   E Cartridge                                                 1
   F Cartridge                                                 1
   G Cartridge                                                 1
   H Cartridge                                                 1
   J Cartridge                                                 1
   K Cartridge                                                 1
*  L Cartridge                                                 1
   M Cartridge                                                 1
   N Cartridge                                                 1
   P Cartridge                                                 1
   Q Cartridge                                                 1

Mark Fonts:  * Present when print job begins        Press Exit to save
                                                  Press Cancel to cancel
```

Figure 3.17 WordPerfect 5.0 printer description—cartridges

```
Select Printer: Cartridges and Fonts

                                          Total Quantity:  2000 K
                                      Available Quantity:   722 K

Soft Fonts                                               Quantity Used

   (AF) Helv 09pt Italic                                       23 K
   (AF) Helv 09pt Italic (Land)                                23 K
   (AF) Helv 11pt                                              27 K
   (AF) Helv 11pt (Land)                                       27 K
   (AF) Helv 11pt Bold                                         28 K
   (AF) Helv 11pt Bold (Land)                                  28 K
   (AF) Helv 11pt Italic                                       28 K
   (AF) Helv 11pt Italic (Land)                                28 K
*  (AF) Helv 18pt                                              55 K
*  (AF) Helv 18pt (Land)                                       55 K
*  (AF) Helv 18pt Italic                                       59 K
   (AF) Helv 18pt Italic (Land)                                59 K
 + (AF) Helv 24pt                                              90 K
 + (AF) Helv 24pt (Land)                                       90 K
 + (AF) Helv 24pt Italic                                       97 K

Mark Fonts:  * Present when print job begins        Press Exit to save
             + Can be loaded during print job     Press Cancel to cancel
```

Figure 3.18 WordPerfect 5.0 printer description—soft fonts

When selecting fonts, you must decide whether the font will always be present in the printer when the print job begins, that is, a *Permanent* font, or can be loaded as required, that is a *Temporary* font. In the case of cartridges, *Present* means that the cartridge must be inserted prior to starting the job. The alternative is to instruct WordPerfect to request the necessary cartridge whenever it needs it. In general, you should define regular cartridge(s) as *Present When the Job Begins* and any secondary cartridges as *Can Be Loaded During Print Job.* The same applies to soft fonts. If you have permanently downloaded a soft font, you can designate it *Present when the Job Begins.* Otherwise, designate any available Temporary soft font as *Can Be Loaded During Print Job.*

Unlike cartridges, Temporary soft fonts will be automatically loaded by WordPerfect as they are needed. When you specify a font as *Present when the Job Begins,* WordPerfect will automatically reduce the amount of available RAM for designating other fonts as *Present when the Job Begins.* This is because Permanent/Present fonts require dedicated printer RAM, while Temporary/Can Be Loaded fonts can share available printer RAM.

Once you have selected the fonts/cartridges available on your printer, you can save the printer definition to your hard disk. You can copy one definition to another printer definition and then edit the second definition to create variations, or you can create several different definitions from scratch. As mentioned above, you will have to experiment with different combinations of definitions to determine which mix of definitions works best for your application.

After setting one or more printer definitions, you can select a particular logical printer from the printer menu by choosing **S** for printer selection. You need only point to the printer definition you wish to use and press **1** or <*Return*> to select it. When you select a printer, remember that it will assume that any *Present when the Job Begins* fonts or cartridges have been properly installed. Thereafter, you can select the Base Font from among the available fonts for the selected printer and can specify any of the available variations from the Font menu, **<CTRL> <F8>**.

Printing on Envelopes

You can either print envelopes through the manual feed of your LaserJet or LaserJet PLUS printer, or with the envelope tray of the LaserJet Series II printer.

Manual

1. Make sure you have a cartridge or soft font that supports a landscape font. The LaserJet Series II and LaserJet 2000 printers have built-in landscape printing capabilities. You must set up the envelope as an available form via the printer definition. Edit the definition by selecting the Edit option after selecting your printer. While in edit mode, select the Forms option, **[4]**, and add the desired envelope size to the available forms (see Figure 3.19). Be sure to leave the Initially Present as "N" and the Location as Manual. Double check; you may have to reset them.

```
Select Printer: Forms
                                   Orient Init             Offset
Form type           Size           P L    Pres Location    Top    Side

Envelope            4" x 9.5"      N Y    N    Manual      0"     0"
Standard            8.5" x 14"     Y Y    N    Manual      0"     0"
Standard            8.5" x 11"     Y Y    Y    Contin      0"     0"
[ALL OTHERS]        Width ≤ 8.5"          N    Manual      0"     0"

If the requested form is not available, then printing stops and WordPerfect
waits for a form to be inserted in the ALL OTHERS location.  If the requested
form is larger than the ALL OTHERS form, the width is set to the maximum width.

1 Add; 2 Delete; 3 Edit: 3
```

Figure 3.19 WordPerfect 5.0 printer description—forms

2. Place or copy the address on a separate page at the end of the document.

3. Select the desired envelop form using the Format menu, **<SHIFT> <F8>**, and choosing the paper size/type option, **[8]**. Note that you must have set up the desired envelope form in step 1 above for it to be available in this step.
4. Press **<SHIFT> <F7>** and select the page print option, **[2]**. The LaserJet will prompt you to insert an envelope.

LaserJet Series II Envelope Tray

To use the optional LaserJet Series II tray with WordPerfect 5.0, you will need to edit your existing LaserJet Series II Printer definition to add the envelope specification.

1. To edit the definition, select it via the Printer Select menu, and chose the edit option **[3]**, (see Figure 3.13).
2. You must now set the Envelope Form to the appropriately sized envelope via the form option, **[4]**.
3. Finally, you must set the form location to Continuous corresponding to the envelope tray. If you specify the tray as being Initially Present, you must insure that it is before you begin to print. If you specify the form as not being initially present, WordPerfect will call for it when needed. You can either feed a single envelope manually or insert the envelope tray.
5. Now when you specify the envelope form via the Format menu, it will look for the envelopes in the envelope tray.

Using Legal-Size Paper

Setting up legal-size paper for both manual and cassette feeding is the same as printing envelopes. The only difference is the substitution of the form specification for legal-size paper for the envelope specification. Again, you must be sure to set the form up first before you can call it from the format menu.

Word 4.0

Microsoft Corporation
16011 NE 36th Way
Redmond, WA 97017

Technical Support: (206) 882-8089
Hours: (M–F) 6:00A.M. – 6:00P.M. PST

Highlights

- Overview
- Installing Your LaserJet Printer with Word
- Changing Fonts Within a Document
- Printing Envelopes
- Changing the Margins
- In Case of Difficulty
- Creating Custom PRDs

Overview

Microsoft Word offers extensive printer control features for the LaserJet printers, offering over 23 printer description files (PRDs) for the LaserJet printer family. These include:

Font Source	*WORD PRD FILE*
Internal Fonts	
LaserJet	HPLASCR.PRD
LaserJet PLUS	HPLASCR2.PRD
LaserJet 500 PLUS	HPLASCR2.PRD
Series II	HPLASCR2.PRD
Font Cartridges	
92286A	HPLASCR.PRD
92286B	HPLASPS.PRD
92286C	HPLASINT.PRD
92286D	HPLASPR.PRD

92286E	HPLASLG.PRD
92286F	HPLASRMN.PRD
92286G	HPLASLPR.PRD
92286H	HPLASLCR.PRD
92286J	HPLASMATH.PRD
92286K	HPMTHTMS.PRD
92286L	HPLASCR2.PRD
92286M	HPLASPR.PRD
92286N	HPLASLG.PRD
92286P	HPLSRMN2.PRD
92286Q	HPLSMEMO.PRD
92286R	Not Supported
92286T	HPLASTAX.PRD
92286U	HPFORMSP.PRD
92286W	HPLSOCRA.PRD
92286X	HPLSOCRB.PRD
92286Y	HPPCCOUR.PRD
92286Z	HPLASMS.PRD
Soft Font	
33412AC (Portrait)	HPDWNSFP.PRD
(Landscape)	HPDWINSFL.PRD
33412AD (Portrait)	HPDWNR8P.ORD
(Landscape)	HPDWNR8L.PRD
33412AE	Not Supported
33412AF	Not Supported
33412DA	Not Supported
33412EA	Not Supported
33412RA	Not Supported
33412SA	Not Supported
33412TA	Not Supported
33412UA	Not Supported

Installing Your LaserJet Printer with Word

Word allows you to install your LaserJet printer with either of two methods.

1. The utilities diskette contains a file called SETUP. When you run it, the program displays easy-to-follow instructions. Simply choose the desired printer definition, and

SETUP will copy the necessary font driver information to your hard disk.

2. Copy all of the LaserJet PRD files to your hard disk, so they are available for use. The only disadvantage with this method is that it wastes space.

> **Note:** If you wish to use a font that Word does not support, you will have to create a custom driver, as described later in this section.

Changing Fonts Within a Document

Whenever you select Print Options from the menu, you can select a PRD file by typing its name. You can also press the right arrow key, which will display all installed PRDs. Move the highlighted cursor to the desired PRD and press <**RETURN**>. The appropriate PRD file will then be loaded, and the printer will use the proper driver.

To select a supported font:

1. Highlight the text to be formatted.
2. Press <**ESC**> Format Character.
3. The following format character options will be displayed:

```
Bold:  yes  no           Italic:  yes  no
Underline:  yes  no  Double Underline: yes no
Position:  Normal  Superscript  Subscript
Font name:               Font size:
```

Bold, *italics*, and underlining are selected by tabbing to the option and then pressing the space bar to highlight either **Yes** or **No**. To select a font, <**TAB**> to Font Name, type the name of the font, then <**TAB**> to Font Size, type the point size of the font, and press <**ENTER**>.

If you don't know the font name or point size, press the <**F1**> key. Word will display the list of supported font names and point sizes. You can then use your arrow keys to highlight the desired selection. Press <**RETURN**> when you are done.

The pages should print out with the desired type font. If not, check the following items:

1. Are you using the correct PRD file?
2. Are your font cartridges seated?
3. If you are using a soft font, has it been downloaded?

Printing Envelopes

To print envelopes, you must embed two escape sequences. For a standard size, #10 envelope:

1. Create a new document.
2. At the very top, enter on the same line the two escape sequences listed for your printer:

   LaserJet Series II

   EcE

   Ec&l1o3h25E

   LaserJet, LaserJet+, LaserJet 500+

   EcE

   Ec&l1o3h38E

Where

EcE resets the printer,

Ec&l1o selects the Landscape orientation,

3h instructs the printer to request a manually fed envelope,

25E and 38E set the printer's top margin to 25 or 38.

Here's how to enter the above codes:

In PCL commands, the number one = 1; the lowercase letter "el" = l; the number zero = 0; and the uppercase letter "oh" = O.

(a) Press and hold the **<ALT>** key, type **27** on the numeric keypad, and then release the **<ALT>** key. An arrow pointing to the left will be displayed.

(b) DON'T type any spaces at this point. Also, enter the escape sequence EXACTLY as it appears above, with no extra spaces. Upper- and lowercase must be exact. Also, be careful to distinguish between lowercase "L" and one, "1".

(c) Press **<RETURN>** after you have finished.

3. To continue with the envelope printing process, press **<ESC>** Format Division Margins. Use the following settings:

Top Margin	0"
Bottom Margin	0"
Left Margin	5.5"
Right Margin	0.5"
Page Length	11"
Page Width	8.5"

4. Now type your addresses, separating each with a page break.
5. Press **<ESC>** Print Options, type **HPLASPLAN** (the PRD for Landscape orientation fonts) and press **<RETURN>.**
6. Turn on the extend selection feature by pressing **<F6>**, then press **<SHIFT>** **<F10>** and highlight the entire document. Now press **<ESC>** Format Character and select the Courier 12 point font.
7. Select **Print**. If you are using a Classic LaserJet, a LaserJet PLUS, or LaserJet 500 PLUS printer, the LED will flash `FE`. With a LaserJet Series II, the LCD will read

```
PE Feed Envelope
```

Insert an envelope into the manual feed slot.

Changing the Margins

If you want to change the left margin of the address so that it falls at a specific location for your envelopes, use the Format Division Margins command. If you want to adjust the top margin, however, you must make your changes within the escape sequence (e.g., **23E** in place of **25E**).

In Case of Difficulty

Envelopes may fail to print for one of two reasons:

1. Your printer does not have landscape fonts.
2. You've entered an incorrect escape sequence (e.g., used a lowercase "e" instead of an uppercase "E"). Re-enter the escape sequence and try again, checking your entry very carefully.

Creating Custom PRDs

If you can't find a PRD file for your soft font or cartridge, you will have to create your own with the MAKEPRD program included with the utilities diskette. Your Word manual explains how to use the program. Alternatively, you can use Font Control™ from Polaris Software, which automatically generates PRD files for HP font cartridges and soft fonts. You can order Font Control from Polaris Software at (800)338-5943, or (800)231-3531 in California.

APPENDIX A

LASERJET SERIES II MEMORY EXPANSION AND OPTION BOARDS

There are hundreds of hardware enhancements for the LaserJet printer family, many of which are listed in *HP LaserJet Printer Family, Software and Hardware Solutions,* periodically updated and free from HP. We have selected several key items to give you a sense of the types of options currently available for your printer, and how they can expand your printing capabilities. These are not exclusive endorsements; many competing brands are high-quality products worthy of investigation. You can use this discussion as a starting point for your evaluations.

Hewlett-Packard Memory Expansion Boards

Manufacturer: Hewlett-Packard
P.O. Box 3640
Sunnyvale, CA 94088-3640
(800) 538-8787
(408) 738-4133

Application: HP LaserJet Series II memory enhancement card

Description

Three boards (1, 2, and 4 megabyte versions) are available to increase the amount of user-accessable RAM on the LaserJet Series II printer. They are easily installable plug-in cards.

Using the Board

The primary purpose for upgrading the memory of the LaserJet Series II is to increase the number of soft fonts or macros that can be downloaded or to increase the size and resolution of graphics that can be printed. To install one of the memory boards, simply insert it into the memory expansion slot on the left side of the printer. No further installation is required. The printer will recognize the presence of the additional memory automatically.

Comments

The addition of the 1 megabyte memory enhancement board will allow you to print full-page 300 × 300 DPI graphics, and is recommended for single-user installations. The 2-megabyte board adds additional capacity for more soft fonts and is recommended for shared-printer installations. The 4-megabyte board is primarily designed for applications, such as desktop publishing, that require a large number of large-point-size soft fonts.

Requirements

HP LaserJet Series II

Notes

The smaller memory boards are not upgradable to larger capacities and must be replaced by new boards if you need to further increase your memory at a later date. Be sure to consider your ultimate requirements when selecting the correct memory expansion board.

JetScript Adapter System

Manufacturer: QMS, Inc.
1 Magnum Pass
Mobile, AL 36608
(800) 633-4300
Also available directly from Hewlett-Packard

Application: PostScript adapter board for LaserJet Series II

Description

The JetScript adapter board adds complete PostScript page-description-language capability to the LaserJet Series II, without interfering with the LaserJet's own PCL capabilities. The system consists of a controller card that is inserted into one of the expansion slots in your computer, a custom adapter card that is inserted in the optional interface slot of the LaserJet Series II printer, a special cable connecting the two cards, and 2 megabytes of software. You must install the hardware and software, by assigning the board one of the parallel ports of the PC. The controller card doesn't actually occupy the parallel port, but does use its name. Generally, the system is assigned to LPT2:.

Each time you start up your computer, the software is loaded onto the controller card, activating the assigned port and the PostScript controller. Thereafter, you can send data to the PostScript printer by directing it to the assigned port. The original HP interface is still connected and available for use. For example, you could have the printer attached to the computer via LPT1: for PCL use and attached to the JetScript controller via the assigned LPT2: port. You can send PCL-controlled print requests to LPT1: and PostScript requests to LPT2:. The PCL connection will take precedence over the JetScript connection.

Using the Board

After installing the adapter card, you can treat the assigned port as if it were connected to a dedicated PostScript printer such as the Apple LaserWriter. You can install the appropriate print drivers (any of the PostScript drivers should work) in your application software and direct output to the assigned port. The original HP interface connection (e.g., COM1: or LPT1:) is still active and can be treated as a separate printer attached to that port. The PCL port takes precedence if two separate requests are sent simultaneously to the printer over both ports.

Comments

This is one of the most useful enhancements you can add to your LaserJet Series II. It truly gives you the best of both the PCL and the PostScript worlds. It is simple to install and extremely easy to use. It was developed with the advice and consent of HP and is offered directly through HP as one of its own upgrade options. The chief advantages of the JetScript adapter system are:

1. The low cost relative to purchasing a dedicated PostScript printer in addition to your existing LaserJet Series II.
2. Your LaserJet Series II retains its PCL capabilities.
3. The PostScript data is transmitted to the printer directly via the computer's high-speed internal bus and the special high-speed cable linking the two JetScript adapter boards.

The only disadvantage of this system is that it requires one of the expansion slots of your computer and it consumes 15 watts, a possible drain on your power supply and a definite heat producer.

Requirements

1. An HP LaserJet Series II printer
2. One full-sized expansion slot in the computer
3. Two megabytes of available disk space

4. DOS 2.0 or higher
5. Nearby desk space. The adapter cable is only 10 feet long.

Notes

QMS also manufacturers PostScript boards for the LaserJet and the LaserJet PLUS.

JLASER Interface Card

Manufacturer: Tall Tree Systems
P.O. Box 50690
Palo Alto, CA 94303
(415) 493-1980

Application: A high-speed printer interface for the HP Series II and other Canon LBP-CX laser printers

Description

The JLASER system consists of a large high-speed print buffer located on an expansion card placed in your computer, an optional interface card placed in the Series II printer, and a special connecting cable and software used to drive the system. The key to the JLASER system is the placement of the print buffer memory directly on the computer's internal bus. This permits software to transfer print instructions directly to the print buffer at the higher internal bus speed rather than the external port speeds. The print buffer then transmits the data to the optional interface card in the printer via the special high-speed connecting cable. The speed improvements are substantial as compared to a serial connection operating at 9,600 baud or even the parallel interface.

The JLASER software also provides support for the additional Series II resident fonts for non-Series II printers, and provides soft font capability for these printers as well. The software also provides additional on-screen font support for many application packages.

Using the Board

After installing the adapter cards and the JLASER software, you must initializie the JLASER port by running the JOUTPUT program. This sets up the printer buffer as the default printer "port," directing all print output to it and thence to the laser printer. You can reset the printer port to the standard HP interface by turning the printer off and on again. By installing your software with the JLASER print driver, you access the additional font and graphics support provided in the software.

Comments

The JLASER card primary benefit is its speed. It is astonishingly fast compared to the standard serial and parallel interfaces. It also affords additional fonts and graphics support to software using its special print drivers. It can be attached to many different printers, though the Series II connection is the easiest. The memory on the JRAM card portion of the JLASER adapter card can also be used for Expanded Memory according to the Lotus-Intel-MicroSoft Expanded Memory Specification.

The only disadvantage of this system is that it requires one of the full-length expansion slots of your computer, and it consumes about 5 watts, a possible drain on your power supply and a definite source of heat. Also, while it is extremely fast as a PCL-based system, it does not offer the benefits of PostScript support afforded by such boards as the JetScript.

Requirements

1. An HP LaserJet Series II or CANON LBP-CX-based printer
2. One full-sized expansion slot in the computer
3. DOS 2.0 or higher
4. Nearby desk space. The adapter cable is only 10 feet long.

ShareSpool

Manufacturer: Extended Systems
6062 Morris Hill
P.O. Box 4937
Boise, ID 83711
(208) 322-7163

Application: An intelligent printer-sharing and spooling system for the HP LaserJet Series II printer

Description

The ShareSpool system is installed in the "I/O option" slot in the back of the LaserJet Series II printer. It contains an internal 256K byte buffer and four connecting ports. Each port can be connected to a separate PC or compatible computer via a serial port. Fifty-foot modular-jack cables and adapters are required and can be supplied by Extended Systems. All four computers can transmit print data simultaneously at speeds up to 19,200 baud. The ShareSpool system will automatically assign buffer space to each job as required. Each job will be printed in the order received. It is also possible to instruct the ShareSpool system to print multiple collated copies of a print job.

Using the Board

After installing the ShareSpool in the "I/O option" slot of the LaserJet Series II and connecting the cables to a serial port on each of the attached computers, you need only configure the computer ports for serial operation at 9,600 or 19,200 baud via the mode commands:

```
MODE COM1:9600,N,8,1,P
MODE LPT1:=COM1:
```

Substitute COM2: or COM3: if appropriate.
Substitute 19200 for 9600 if appropriate.
Thereafter, all print jobs will be automatically directed to the ShareSpool connection and printed in the order received. It is possible to issue special ShareSpool commands to control the number of copies, multiple copy printing priority, and so on.

Comments

The Extended Systems' ShareSpool is much more than a smart switch box. It contains built-in print buffering and the logic necessary to separate print jobs. The modular-jack cabling is not supplied with the product, but everything necessary is available from Extended Systems. Be sure to specify the connections needed when ordering (25 pin for PCs and XTs and 9 pin for ATs, etc.). Also, the system supports cable lengths up to 200 feet, which is a definite plus when you consider that the desks of many multiple-user environments are spaced widely apart.

Requirements

1. An HP LaserJet Series II printer
2. One serial port on each computer

JetMemory

Manufacturer: Computer Peripherals Inc.
667 Rancho Conejo Blvd.
Newbury Park, CA 91320
(805) 499-5751
(800) 854-7600

Application: HP LaserJet Series II memory enhancement card

Description

The JetMemory is a substitute for the HP memory upgrade cards and is functionally identical. In contrast to the HP memory boards, the JetMemory series is modular in design, allowing you to start with only 1 megabyte and later adding an additional 1 or 3 megabytes. With the HP boards, you must replace the smaller boards with one of the larger ones to upgrade your memory a second time.

Using the Board

The primary purpose for upgrading the memory of the LaserJet Series II printer is to increase the number of soft fonts or macros that can be downloaded or to increase the size and resolution of graphics that can be printed. To install one of the memory boards, simply insert it into the memory expansion slot on the left side of the printer. No further installation is required. The printer will recognize the presence of the additional memory automatically.

Comments

The primary advantage of the JetMemory expansion memory boards is their modular design, which allows you to upgrade the base 1 megabyte board to either 2 or 4 megabytes in the future.

There also may be some difference in cost as compared to purchasing the boards from HP. You will have to judge the value of the modular design and potential cost savings based on your particular requirements.

Requirements

An HP LaserJet Series II

JetFont 123 and JetFont Four-in-One Font Cartridges

Manufacturer: Computer Peripherals Inc.
667 Rancho Conejo Blvd.
Newbury Park, CA 91320
(805) 499-5751
(800) 854-7600

Application: Special-purpose and expanded-purpose font cartridges

Description

The JetFont 123 cartridge contains a series of small and very small fixed-pitch fonts useful for printing large worksheets from your spreadsheet program or reports from you database program. The quite legible Lotica 30-pitch font is capable of printing up to 390 columns of text on a legal sheet of paper in Landscape mode, although some software products (e.g., Lotus 1-2-3) have lower limits.

The four-in-one cartridge contains the common Courier, Prestige Elite, and Letter Gothic fonts, including Medium, Bold, and Italic in Portrait orientation.

Usage

The four-in-one font cartridge is best suited for common word processing, while the 1-2-3 cartridge is best suited for spreadsheets and database applications. The fonts are specified by their characteristics in the same fashion as the regular HP fonts. You can use the programs on the Laser-ToolKit Utility Disk to access the Lotica fonts from this cartridge from within several common application programs.

Comments

The four-in-one cartridge contains the most common word processing fonts that would require several of the HP font cartridge to duplicate (the HP cartridges contain other fonts as well those contained on the four-in-one). The Lotica typeface used on the extremely small type of the 1-2-3 cartridge is remarkably legible. It produces a much better result than printing in a larger format and then reducing the output xerographically.

Requirements

HP LaserJet, LaserJet PLUS, or LaserJet Series II

APPENDIX B

GLOSSARY

AUTO CONTINUE: A feature on the LaserJet Series II that allows the printer to continue operating despite an error message.

BAUD RATE: A measure of the speed at which data are transferred serially. LaserJets can be configured to receive data at speeds of between 300 and 19,200 baud.

BIT MAPPING: The process by which characters are described graphically as a series of 1s and 0s, which corresponds to dots and white spaces.

BOND PAPER: Any paper that consists of pure cellulose or cotton fiber.

C5: Envelopes that measure 162mm × 229mm.

COM-10: Commercial size (#10) envelope. Standard business size, 4½ × 9½.

CONFIGURATION: A setting that determines whether the printer is set up to receive data via a serial or a parallel interface.

COTTON BOND: Paper that consists of fibers made from rags. It has the finest feel and is generally used for letterhead stationery. Since it does not have the optimal electrical properties and tends to jam in mechanical feeders, it is not recommended for laser printers.

CPI: Characters per inch, also known as *pitch*.

DDL: Stands for *Document Description Language.* DDL was created by Imagen Corporation and Xerox Corporation to control laser printers. It is similar to and competitive with PostScript. Some laser printers can support both page description languages.

DEFAULT: A feature setting that is used each time the printer is turned on.

DECIPOINT A unit of measurement used by the LaserJet for spacing characters and graphics, equal to 1/720th of an inch.

DL: Refers to envelopes that measure 110mm × 220mm.

DOWNLOADING: A process in which soft fonts stored on a disk are transferred to the printer.

DTR POLARITY: The printer constantly emits a DTR (Data Terminal Ready) signal to the computer to indicate whether it is ready to receive data. Normally, high DTR polarity indicates that the printer buffer is empty, while low DTR tells the computer the buffer is full, and data transmission should be suspended.

EP CARTRIDGE: A disposable electrophotographic cartridge that contains a supply of toner, a light-sensitive drum, a charging wire, and a cleaning assembly.

ESCAPE CHARACTER: The nonprinting control character assigned to the decimal ASCII number 027. Used by the HP LaserJets and most other printers to indicate the beginning of a printer command.

ESCAPE SEQUENCE: A printer command beginning with the Escape Character.

FACTORY DEFAULT: A group of settings programmed into the printer's permanent ROM memory during manufacture. The settings can be changed by altering dip switches on the classic LaserJet/LaserJet PLUS/LaserJet 500 PLUS printers, or overridden on the LaserJet Series II by changing the User Defaults via the Control Panel Menu System.

FONT: A group of characters and symbols related by certain criteria (weight, style, pitch, etc). Fonts are available from three sources:

1. Resident—programmed into the printer's memory
2. Plug-in cartridges
3. Disk-based soft fonts

FUSER ASSEMBLY: A mechanism consisting of two high-temperature rollers that melt the toner onto the paper, forming a permanent image.

HORIZONTAL MOTION INDEX (HMI): Defines the distance between characters, measured in 1/120th of an inch.

INTERNAL FONTS: The fonts that are programmed into the printer's memory at the factory. These are also called resident fonts.

I/O: An abbreviation for *Input/Output*, which refers to a device's interface (i.e., serial or parallel connection).

I/O BUFFER: The portion of the printer's memory that first stores the data when they are transmitted from the computer.

LASER: A highly focused monochromatic light source used to scan across the photosensitive drum. The laser pulses on or off in a pattern corresponding to the image on the page.

LANDSCAPE ORIENTATION: Widthwise, or sideways, printing. Contrast with Portrait, or lengthwise, printing.

LOGICAL PAGE: The portion of the page that can be printed (as distinct from the physical page).

MACRO: A series of commands that are stored together so they can be easily recalled and rerun.

MONARC: Designation for envelopes sized 3 7/8 × 7 1/2.

OFFLINE: A status in which the printer cannot accept data.

ONLINE: Ready mode, in which the printer can accept data from the computer.

PAGE-DESCRIPTION LANGUAGE: A specialty language used to tell page printers such as the LaserJet how to position and print characters and graphics. PostScript and DDL are common page-description languages.

PAGE ORIENTATION: Refers to whether a font will print in Portrait or Landscape orientation.

PAPER GRAIN: The direction of the fibers in paper. For laser printing, long (lengthwise) grain is recommended.

PAGE PRINTER: Printers that compose and print entire pages as contrasted with line printers, which print one line at a time.

PAPER PATH: The mechanism that guides the paper from the tray or manual feed through the imaging and fuser assemblies.

PARALLEL INTERFACE: A communications channel between a computer and external peripheral devices such as printers, generally referred to as LPT1: or LPT2:, in which data are transmitted eight bits at a time over eight seperate data lines.

PCL: An abbreviation for *Printer Command Language.* PCL commands are used to change margins, fonts, and other page formatting options.

PITCH: The number of characters per inch (cpi).

POINT SIZE: The height of a character, measured in 1/72 of an inch.

PORTRAIT ORIENTATION: Lengthwise printing.

POSTSCRIPT: A powerful page-description language developed by Adobe Systems Incorporated, used to print a wide variety of type fonts and graphics on a laser printer or phototypesetter.

PRIMARY CORONA WIRE: A wire in the EP cartridge that places a uniform electrical charge on the photosensitive drum, so that it will repell toner except in the areas discharged by the laser.

PRINT DENSITY: The darkness of the print as it is laid down on the paper. The darker the print density, the quicker the toner will be used up.

PRINT DRIVER: A file used to tell an application program how to control a particular printer. With printers that can be altered by adding font cartridges or soft fonts, such as the LaserJet, more than one print driver may be required.

RAM: Random Access Memory (RAM) is high-speed memory in both computers and printers used to temporarily store data. RAM memory is lost when the printer or computer is turned off.

ROM: Read Only Memory (ROM) is permanent memory used in computers and printers to store programs, data, and default settings that can be read but never altered. Unlike RAM memory, ROM memory is not lost when the device is turned off.

RASTERIZATION: A process by which graphic elements are converted into dots. This is equivalent to bit mapping.

RESOLUTION: The measurement of the precision of a printing device such as a laser printer measured in Dots Per Inch (DPI). The HP LaserJets can print with 300 DPI resolution. Resolution can also be used to describe the DPI used to print a particular graphic element.

ROBUST-XON: A "handshaking" signal that the printer sends to the computer to indicate whether it is ready to receive data.

SOFT FONT: Font images stored on a disk. Soft fonts must be downloaded to the printer before they can be used.

SANS-SERIF TYPEFACE: A typeface without serifs, such as Helvetica (see serifs).

SERIAL INTERFACE: A communications channel between a computer and external peripheral devices such as printers, modems, and other computers, in which data are transmitted sequentially one bit at time over a single data line. It is generally referred to as COM1:, COM2:, or COM3:, The speed of a serial interface is measured in baud rates. LaserJets use 9,600 baud as the default speed for serial interfaces.

SERIF TYPEFACE: A typeface that has fine horizontal strokes on the ascenders and descenders. The serifs help guide the eye along a line of type, and make the typeface more suitable for blocks of text than sans-serif faces. Times Roman is a typical serif typeface.

STATUS INDICATOR: Feedback from the printer, in the form of a code or message (LaserJet Series II) describing the operating conditions of the printer (e.g., `02 – WARM UP`).

STROKE WEIGHT: The thickness of the strokes making up a character. The traditional stroke weights are light, medium (also called regular), and bold.

STYLE: Refers to whether a typeface is upright (regular or Roman) or slanted (italic).

SYMBOL SET: The entire set of characters that comprise a font, including letters, numbers, and special symbols. Symbols include such characters as accent marks and the legal paragraph symbol. Symbol sets are available for various foreign languages and specialized purposes, such as legal or mathematical typing.

TONER: A plastic-based powdered ink with a magnetic core. The toner is first attracted to the drum in the EP cartridge, and then transferred to the paper. The fuser assembly melts the toner into the paper, forming the permanent image.

TRANSFER CORONA WIRE: A thin steel wire that produces a uniform electrical charge on the paper before it passes into the imaging assembly. This charge enables the paper to attract the toner from the EP drum.

TYPEFACE: A unique character design, such as Courier, Times Roman, Helvetica, and so on.

USER DEFAULT ENVIRONMENT: LaserJet Series II printer settings that a user enters via the Control Panel Menu System.

VERTICAL MOTION INDEX: A measure of the spacing between lines, measured in 1/48th of an inch.

XEROGRAPHIC PAPER: A type of bond paper with the best electrical properties for laser printing. It is precisely cut, and is made for high-speed mechanical feeding.

APPENDIX C

FONT SHOWCASE

TmsRmn

abcdefghijklmnopqrstuvwxyz
ABCDEFGHIJKLMNOPQRSTUVWXYZ

6 Type has personality. Choose the face that reflects and complements
the information you're communicating. Be sparing in your use of

7 Type has personality. Choose the face that reflects and compl
ements the information you're communicating. Be sparing in

8 Type has personality. Choose the face that reflects and
complements the information you're communicating.

9 Type has personality. Choose the face that reflec
ts and complements the information you're com

10 Type has personality. Choose the face that
reflects and complements the information y

11 Type has personality. Choose the face
that reflects and complements the info

12 Type has personality. Choose the
face that reflects and complements

14 Type has personality. Choose the
face that reflects the information y

18 Type has personality. Cho
ose the face that reflects an

24 Type has personali
ty. Choose the face

30 Type has person
ality. Choose th

---

abcdefghijklmnopqrstuvwxyz
ABCDEFGHIJKLMNOPQRSTUVWXYZ

6 *Type has personality. Choose the face that reflects and complements the*
information you're communicating. Be sparing in your use of different

7 *Type has personality. Choose the face that reflects and co*
mplements the information you're communicating. Be sparing

8 *Type has personality. Choose the face that reflects and*
complements the information you're communicating. B

9 *Type has personality. Choose the face that reflects*
and complements the information you're commu

10 *Type has personality. Choose the face that ref*
lects and complements the information you'r

11 *Type has personality. Choose the face th*
at reflects and complements the informa

12 *Type has personality. Choose the fa*
ce that reflects and complements the

14 *Type has personality. Choose the fa*
ce that reflects the information you're

18 *Type has personality. Choo*
se the face that reflects and c

24 *Type has personality.*
Choose the face that r

30 *Type has person*
ality. Choose the

Headlines

abcdefghijklmnopqrstuvwxyz
ABCDEFGHIJKLMNOPQRSTUVWXYZ

14 Type has personality. Choose the face that reflects and complements the info

18 Type has personality. Choose the face that reflects and com

24 Type has personality. Choose the face that re

30 Type has personality. Choose the fa

---

abcdefghijklmnopqrstuvwxyz
ABCDEFGHIJKLMNOPQRSTUVWXYZ

14 Type has personality. Choose the face that reflects

18 Type has personality. Choose the face t

24 Type has personality. Choose

30 Type has personality. C

Helv Headlines

abcdefghijklmnopqrstuvwxyz
ABCDEFGHIJKLMNOPQRSTUVWXYZ

14 Type has personality. Choose the face that reflects and com

18 Type has personality. Choose the face that ref

24 Type has personality. Choose the

30 Type has personality. Choo

36 Type has personality.

48 Type has person

---

abcdefghijklmnopqrstuvwxyz
ABCDEFGHIJKLMNOPQRSTUVWXYZ

14 Type has personality. Choose the face that reflects and

18 Type has personality. Choose the face that

24 Type has personality. Choose th

30 Type has personality. Cho

36 Type has personality.

48 Type has perso

ITC Garamond

abcdefghijklmnopqrstuvwxyz
ABCDEFGHIJKLMNOPQRSTUVWXYZ

6 Type has personality. Choose the face that reflects and complements the information you're communicating. Be sparing in your use of

7 Type has personality. Choose the face that reflects and com plements the information you're communicating. Be spari

8 Type has personality. Choose the face that reflects and complements the information you're commun

9 Type has personality. Choose the face that ref lects and complements the information you'r

10 Type has personality. Choose the face that reflects and complements the information

11 Type has personality. Choose the fac that reflects and complements the in

12 Type has personality. Choose the face that reflects and complement

14 Type has personality. Choose th face that reflects the information

18 Type has personality. Cho ose the face that reflects an

24 Type has personali ty. Choose the face

30 Type has pers onality. Choos

---

abcdefghijklmnopqrstuvwxyz
ABCDEFGHIJKLMNOPQRSTUVWXYZ

6 *Type has personality. Choose the face that reflects and complements the information you're communicating. Be sparing in your use of*

7 *Type has personality. Choose the face that reflects and complements the information you're communicating. Be*

8 *Type has personality. Choose the face that reflects and complements the information you're commun*

9 *Type has personality. Choose the face that reflects and complements the information yo*

10 *Type has personality. Choose the face that reflects and complements the infor*

11 *Type has personality. Choose the fac that reflects and complements the in*

12 *Type has personality. Choose the face that reflects and complemen*

14 *Type has personality. Choose th face that reflects the information*

18 *Type has personality. Cho ose the face that reflects th*

24 *Type has personali ty. Choose the face*

30 *Type has perso nality. Use the*

APPENDIX D
SYMBOL SETS

The Hewlett-Packard Symbol Sets

7-Bit Sets:

ASCII*	!	"	#	$	%	&	'	(	)	*	+	,	-	.	/	0	1	2	3	4	5	6	7	8	9
ROMAN EXT.*	À	Â	È	Ê	Ë	Î	Ï	´	`	ˆ	¨	˜	Ù	Û	£	¯	(Ý)	(ý)	°	Ç	ç	Ñ	ñ	¡	¿
FRENCH	!	"	£	$	%	&	'	(	)	*	+	,	-	.	/	0	1	2	3	4	5	6	7	8	9
GERMAN	!	"	£	$	%	&	'	(	)	*	+	,	-	.	/	0	1	2	3	4	5	6	7	8	9
ITALIAN	!	"	£	$	%	&	'	(	)	*	+	,	-	.	/	0	1	2	3	4	5	6	7	8	9
SPANISH	!	"	#	$	%	&	'	(	)	*	+	,	-	.	/	0	1	2	3	4	5	6	7	8	9
SWE/FIN	!	"	#	¤	%	&	'	(	)	*	+	,	-	.	/	0	1	2	3	4	5	6	7	8	9
DAN/NOR	!	"	#	$	%	&	'	(	)	*	+	,	-	.	/	0	1	2	3	4	5	6	7	8	9
U.K.	!	"	£	$	%	&	'	(	)	*	+	,	-	.	/	0	1	2	3	4	5	6	7	8	9
LEGAL	!	″	#	$	%	&	′	(	)	*	+	,	-	.	/	0	1	2	3	4	5	6	7	8	9
LINE DRAW	┣	┫	┳	┻	╟	╢	╤	╧	║	╂	┿	─	└	│	┼	╋	┣	┫	┳	┻	├	┤	┬	┴	=
TAX L.DRAW	┣	┫	┳	┻	╟	╢	╤	╧	║	╂	┿	─	└	│	┼	╋	┣	┫	┳	┻	├	┤	┬	┴	=
MATH-7	√	|	§	∇	±	∝	⌠	÷	≃	Π	Γ	Ψ	▪	Φ	Ξ	^{0}	^{1}	^{2}	^{3}	^{4}	^{5}	^{6}	^{7}	^{8}	^{9}
MATH-8A*	√	″	•	∞	÷	∝	′	(	)	×	+	,	-	.	/	0	1	2	3	4	5	6	7	8	9
MATH-8B*	↑	→	↓	←	⇑	⇒	⇓	⇐	↕	↔	⇕	⇔	≡	≈	⃗	‾	∀	∃	⊤	⊥	∪	∩	∈	∋	∉
PI FONT-A				“	”	‘	’	⟨	⟩	™	℠	®	©	☺		‾	ˉ	ˉ	·	↗	↘	↙	↖	△	▷
OCR-A	!	"	#	$	%	&	'	(	)	*	+	,	-	.	/	0	1	2	3	4	5	6	7	8	9
BAR 3-OF-9				▮	▮					▮	▮	▮	▮	▮	▮	▮	▮	▮	▮	▮	▮	▮	▮	▮	▮
BAR EAN/UPC								▮	▮	▮	▮		▮			▮	▮	▮	▮	▮	▮	▮	▮	▮	▮
OCR-B	!	"	#	$	%	&	'	(	)	*	+	,	-	.	/	0	1	2	3	4	5	6	7	8	9
OCR-B EXT.								´	`	ˆ	¨	˜	.									Ñ			
PC LINE																	░	▒	│	┤	╡	╢	╖	╕	╣

ASCII*	:	;	<	=	>	?	@	A	B	C	D	E	F	G	H	I	J	K
ROMAN EXT.*	¤	£	¥	§	ƒ	¢	â	ê	ô	û	á	é	ó	ú	à	è	ò	ù
FRENCH	:	;	<	=	>	?	à	A	B	C	D	E	F	G	H	I	J	K
GERMAN	:	;	<	=	>	?	§	A	B	C	D	E	F	G	H	I	J	K
ITALIAN	:	;	<	=	>	?	§	A	B	C	D	E	F	G	H	I	J	K
SPANISH	:	;	<	=	>	?	@	A	B	C	D	E	F	G	H	I	J	K
SWE/FIN	:	;	<	=	>	?	É	A	B	C	D	E	F	G	H	I	J	K
DAN/NOR	:	;	<	=	>	?	@	A	B	C	D	E	F	G	H	I	J	K
U.K.	:	;	<	=	>	?	@	A	B	C	D	E	F	G	H	I	J	K
LEGAL	:	;	_	–	¢	?	@	A	B	C	D	E	F	G	H	I	J	K
LINE DRAW	┃	━	╫	┌	╪	╬	╞	┗	╂	█	▌	│	└	┘	┐	┐	┬	┌
TAX L.DRAW	┃	━	╫	┌	╪	╬	╞	┗	╂	█	▌	┃	└	┘	┆	┐	└	┘
MATH-7	Ω	Λ	∞	⌡	†	Σ	¶	α	β	ψ	φ	ε	∂	λ	η	ι	θ	κ
MATH-8A*	ℯ	ε	<	–	>	≈	∴	A	B	Γ	Δ	E	Z	H	Θ	I	K	Λ
MATH-8B*	⊂	⊃	⊄	⊅	⊆	⊇	⊕	⊙	⊗	⊖	⊘	∧	∨	⊻	¬	∘	·	•
PI FONT-A	▽	◁	◀	§	▶	¶	∷	△					ƒ		ħ			
OCR-A	:	;	<	=	>	?	@	A	B	C	D	E	F	G	H	I	J	K
BAR 3-OF-9								▮	▮	▮	▮	▮	▮	▮	▮	▮	▮	▮
BAR EAN/UPC								▮	▮	▮	▮	▮	▮	▮	▮	▮	▮	
OCR-B	:	;	<	=	>	?	@	A	B	C	D	E	F	G	H	I	J	K
OCR-B EXT.	¤	£	¥	§												Ĳ		
PC LINE	║	╗	╝	╜	╛	┐	└	┴	┬	├	─	┼	╞	╟	╚	╔	╩	╦

○ **NOTE: The circled characters are available with the HP33411EA/ HP33412EA soft font product only.**

L	M	N	O	P	Q	R	S	T	U	V	W	X	Y	Z	[	\	]	^	_	'	a	b	c	d	e	f	g	h	i	j	k	l	m	n	o	p	q	r	s	t	u	v	w	x	y	z	{	|	}	~	▒
ä	ë	ö	ü	Å	î	Ø	Æ	å	í	ø	æ	Ä	ì	Ö	Ü	É	ï	ß	Ô	Á	Ã	ã	Đ	đ	Í	Ì	Ó	Ò	Õ	õ	Š	š	Ú	Ÿ	ÿ	Þ	þ	·	µ	¶	¾	–	¼	½	ª	º	«	■	»	±	
L	M	N	O	P	Q	R	S	T	U	V	W	X	Y	Z	°	ç	§	^	_	'	a	b	c	d	e	f	g	h	i	j	k	l	m	n	o	p	q	r	s	t	u	v	w	x	y	z	é	ù	è		■
L	M	N	O	P	Q	R	S	T	U	V	W	X	Y	Z	Ä	Ö	Ü	^	_	'	a	b	c	d	e	f	g	h	i	j	k	l	m	n	o	p	q	r	s	t	u	v	w	x	y	z	ä	ö	ü	ß	■
L	M	N	O	P	Q	R	S	T	U	V	W	X	Y	Z	°	ç	é	^	_	ù	a	b	c	d	e	f	g	h	i	j	k	l	m	n	o	p	q	r	s	t	u	v	w	x	y	z	à	ò	è	ì	■
L	M	N	O	P	Q	R	S	T	U	V	W	X	Y	Z	¡	Ñ	¿	°	_	'	a	b	c	d	e	f	g	h	i	j	k	l	m	n	o	p	q	r	s	t	u	v	w	x	y	z	(	ñ	)	~	▒
L	M	N	O	P	Q	R	S	T	U	V	W	X	Y	Z	Ä	Ö	Å	Ü	_	é	a	b	c	d	e	f	g	h	i	j	k	l	m	n	o	p	q	r	s	t	u	v	w	x	y	z	ä	ö	å	ü	▒
L	M	N	O	P	Q	R	S	T	U	V	W	X	Y	Z	Æ	Ø	Å	^	_	'	a	b	c	d	e	f	g	h	i	j	k	l	m	n	o	p	q	r	s	t	u	v	w	x	y	z	æ	ø	å	~	▒
L	M	N	O	P	Q	R	S	T	U	V	W	X	Y	Z	[	\	]	^	_	'	a	b	c	d	e	f	g	h	i	j	k	l	m	n	o	p	q	r	s	t	u	v	w	x	y	z	{	|	}	~	■
L	M	N	O	P	Q	R	S	T	U	V	W	X	Y	Z	[	®	]	©	_	•	a	b	c	d	e	f	g	h	i	j	k	l	m	n	o	p	q	r	s	t	u	v	w	x	y	z	§	¶	-	™	▫
m	╋	┿	╡	┘	┏	┌	┛	┐	┤	╋	┓	█	┐	▄	╡	··	╨	·	π	╞	┗	╋	█	▌	│	└	┘	¬	┤	┬	∩	m	╋	┿	╡	┘	┏	┌	┛	┐·	┤	╋	┓	█	┐	▄	╡	··	╨	·	
│	╋	┿	─	┘	┏	┌	┛	┐	┌	╋	┓	█	┐	▄	╡	··	╨	·	π	┬	↓	┘	⋮	⋮	⊥	□	▯		┤	▶	◣	◤	⊥	_	┬	┴	↑	-	←	_	├	└	→	│	┼	│	█	•		┴	
ω	μ	ν	ρ	π	γ	θ	σ	τ	ξ	Δ	δ	χ	υ	ς	↑	→	T	←	↓	¶	α	β	ψ	φ	ε	∂	λ	η	ι	Θ	κ	ω	μ	ν	ρ	π	γ	θ	σ	τ	ξ	Δ	δ	χ	υ	ς	↑	→	T	←	▒
M	N	Ξ	O	Π	P	Σ	T	T	Φ	X	Ψ	Ω	∇	∂	ς	≤	≠	≥	_	∵	α	β	γ	δ	ε	ζ	η	θ	ι	κ	λ	μ	ν	ξ	ο	π	ρ	σ	τ	υ	φ	χ	ψ	ω	ϑ	φ	ϖ	≃	≡	≢	▒
•	○	†	‡	Å	⊣	⊢			∫	∮	∠	∅	ℵ	⊃	⊂	ℭ	ℨ	ℜ	3	⌈	⌊	⎧	⎨	⎩	⌠	ϕ	⌡	⎲	‖	∠	/					⎤	⎦	⎫	⎬	⎭	│	│	⌡	¯	〉	_	\		∓	±	
ℒ	ℓ			℘	℘	ℜ	∑								⟦	‖	⟧			┌	└	╭	╰	┼	├	─	‖	∪	∩	⟦	⟦	□	◇			┐	┘	╮	╯	┬	┤	┴	│	⊔	⊓	⁞	‖	■	♦		▒
L	M	N	O	P	Q	R	S	T	U	V	W	X	Y	Z	[	\	]	^	⑂	⑀	a	b	c	d	e	f	g	h	i	j	k	l	m	n	o	p	q	r	s	t	u	v	w	x	y	z	{	|	}	⑁	■
▮	▮	▮	▮	▮	▮	▮	▮	▮	▮	▮	▮	▮	▮	▮																																					
																					▮	▮	▮	▮	▮	▮	▮	▮	▮	▮																					
L	M	N	O	P	Q	R	S	T	U	V	W	X	Y	Z	[	\	]	^	_		a	b	c	d	e	f	g	h	i	j	k	l	m	n	o	p	q	r	s	t	u	v	w	x	y	z	{	|	}		■
				Å		Ø	Æ	å		ø	æ	Ä		Ö	Ü			ß											ĳ																						
╟	═	╬	╧	╨	╤	╥	╙	╘	╒	╓	╫	╪	┘	┌	█	▄	▌	▐	▀																										•	·				▪	

ABOUT THE AUTHORS

Peter G. Randall is president of Ariel Enterprises, Inc., a software development and consulting firm. Prior to the start-up of Ariel, he served as president of ESIS International, an international marketing subsidiary of Cigna Corporation. Mr. Randall, who holds a BSE in systems engineering from Princeton University and an MBA from the Wharton School of Business, has written more than 30 major application programs for use in business. He has co-authored *1-2-3 Ready-To-Run, dBASE III Plus To Go, The HAL Handbook, 1-2-3 Power Pack, WordPerfect Power Pack, Instant Byline,* and *Instant Pagemaker* (all published by Brady).

Steven J. Bennett is a professional writer and computer consultant. Educated at the University of Rochester and Harvard University, he has edited and written numerous medical and scientific publications, and has authored a number of business books, including *Playing Hardball with Soft Skills* (Bantam), *Executive Chess* (New American Library), and *Think To Win* (New American Library). He has also co-authored eight computer books: *1-2-3 Ready-To-Run, dBASE III Plus To Go, The HAL Handbook, 1-2-3 Power Pack, WordPerfect Power Pack, Instant Byline, Instant Pagemaker,* and *Instant Ventura Publisher* (all published by Brady).

PETER G. RANDALL

STEVEN J. BENNETT

INDEX

CUSTOMER SUPPORT

It is important that you register your purchase of any Simon & Schuster software package. By completing and returning your Owner Registration Card, you become eligible for:

- Software support directly from S & S.
- Diskette replacement when applicable.
- Purchase of future product upgrades at special prices.
- Subscriptions to Hint Books and newsletters where applicable.

Software Support

S & S will provide support to registered owners. Our technical support number is (900) 370-2550. It is staffed on working days during normal business hours, 10:00 am to 6:00 pm, Eastern time. There is a charge of $1.00 per minute charged to your phone for each minute after the first.

Mail-in Support Service—Registered owners may write to us with questions. We will respond in writing. There is no additional charge for this service.

We realize that our software packages are put to a wide variety of uses, however, we can only answer questions about the software package itself. We cannot support the hardware and operating system required to run our software packages.

Before Calling Customer Support

Before calling our Technical Support Department, please make sure you have followed the steps in the "Pre-call Checklist" below.

Pre-call Checklist

1. If you are having difficulty understanding the program, have you read and performed the suggestions listed in the manual?

2. If you are not sure how to operate the program, have you used the help system (where available) to find the answer?

3. If there seems to be a problem in the software, can you reproduce the problem by following your steps again?

4. If the program displayed an error message, please write down the exact message.

5. You should be familiar with the hardware configuration you are using. We may need to know the brand/model of your computer, printer, the total amount of memory available, what video adaptor(s) you have in the system, the operating system version, etc.

6. When you call our Technical Support Department, please be at your computer or be prepared to repeat the sequence of steps leading up to the problem.

Services and Prices

The above services and prices are subject to change without prior notice.

Important! Read Before Opening Sealed Diskette
END USER LICENSE AGREEMENT

The software in this package is provided to You on the condition that You agree with SIMON & SCHUSTER, INC. ("S&S") to the terms and conditions set forth below. **Read this End User Agreement carefully. You will be bound by the terms of this agreement if you open the sealed diskette.** If You do not agree to the terms contained in this End User License Agreement, return the entire product, along with your receipt, to *Brady, Simon & Schuster, Inc., One Gulf + Western Plaza, New York, NY 10023, Attn: Refunds,* and your purchase price will be refunded.

S&S grants, and You hereby accept, a personal, nonexclusive license to use the software program and associated documentation in this package, or any part of it ("Licensed Product"), subject to the following terms and conditions:

1. *License*

The license granted to You hereunder authorizes You to use the Licensed Product on any single computer system. A separate license, pursuant to a separate End User License Agreement, is required for any other computer system on which You intend to use the Licensed Product.

2. *Term*

This End User License Agreement is effective from the date of purchase by You of the Licensed Product and shall remain in force until terminated. You may terminate this End User License Agreement at any time by destroying the Licensed Product together with all copies in any form made by You or received by You. Your right to use or copy the Licensed Product will terminate if You fail to comply with any of the terms or conditions of this End User License Agreement. Upon such termination You shall destroy the copies of the Licensed Product in your possession.

3. *Restriction Against Transfer*

This End User License Agreement, and the Licensed Product, may not be assigned, sublicensed or otherwise transfered by You to another party unless the other party agrees to accept the terms and conditions of this End User License Agreement. If You transfer the Licensed Product, You must at the same time either transfer all copies whether in printed or machine-readable form to the same party or destroy any copies not transferred.

4. *Restrictions Against Copying or Modifying the Licensed Product*

The Licensed Product is copyrighted and except for certain limited uses as noted on the copyright page, may not be further copied without the prior written approval of S&S, except that You may make one copy for backup purposes provided You reproduce and include the complete copyright notice on the backup copy. Any unauthorized copying is in violation of this Agreement and may also constitute a violation of the United States Copyright Law for which You could be liable in a civil or criminal suit. **You may not use, transfer, copy or otherwise reproduce the Licensed Product, or any part of it, except as expressly permitted in this End User License Agreement.**

5. *Protection and Security*

You shall take all reasonable steps to safeguard the Licensed Product and to ensure that no unauthorized person shall have access to it and that no unauthorized copy of any part of it in any form shall be made.

6. **Limited Warranty**

If You are the original consumer purchaser of a diskette and its found to be defective in materials or workmanship (which shall not include problems relating to the nature or operation of the Licensed Product) under normal use, S&S will replace it free of charge (or, at S&S's option, refund your purchase price) within 30 days following the date of purchase. Following the 30-day period, and up to one year after purchase, S&S will replace any such defective diskette upon payment of a $5 charge (or, at S&S's option, refund your purchase price), provided that the Limited Warranty Registration Card has been filed within 30 days following the date of purchase. Any request for replacement of a defective diskette must be accompanied by the original defective diskette and proof of date of purchase and purchase price. S&S shall have no obligation to replace a diskette (or refund your purchase price) based on claims of defects in the nature or operation of the Licensed Product.

The software program is provided "as is" without warranty of any kind, either expressed or implied, including but not limited to the implied warranties of merchantability and fitness for a particular purpose. The entire risk as to the quality and performance of the program is with You. Should the program prove defective, You (and not S&S) assume the entire cost of all necessary servicing, repair or correction.

Some states do not allow the exclusion of implied warranties, so the above exclusion may not apply to You. This warrant gives You specific legal rights, and You may also have other rights which vary from state to state.

S&S does not warrant that the functions contained in the program will meet your requirements or that the operation of the program will be uninterrupted or error free. Neither S&S nor anyone else who has been involved in the creation or production of this product shall be liable for any direct, indirect, incidental, special or consequential damages, whether arising out of the use or inability to use the product, or any breach of a warranty, and S&S shall have no responsibility except to replace the diskette pursuant to this limited warranty (or, at its option, provide a refund of the purchase price).

No sales personnel or other representative of any party involved in the distribution of the Licensed Product is authorized by S&S to make any warranties with respect to the diskette or the Licensed Product beyond those contained in this Agreement. **Oral statements do not constitute warranties,** shall not be relied upon by You, and are not part of this Agreement. The entire agreement between S&S and You is embodied in this Agreement.

7. *General*

If any provision of this End User License Agreement is determined to be invalid under any applicable statute of rule of law, it shall be deemed omitted and the remaining provisions shall continue in full force and effect. This End User License Agreement is to be governed by the construed in accordance with the laws of the State of New York.

Hewlett-Packard Laser Printer Power Pack

REPLACEMENT ORDER FORM

Please use this form when ordering a replacement for a defective diskette.

A. If Ordering within Thirty Days of Purchase
If a diskette is reported defective within thirty days of purchase, a replacement diskette will be provided free of charge. *This card must be totally filled out and accompanied by the defective diskette and a copy of the dated sales receipt.* In addition, please complete and return the Limited Warranty Registration Card.

B. If Ordering after Thirty Days of Purchase but within One Year
If a diskette is reported defective after thirty days, but within one year of purchase and the Warranty Registration Card has been properly filed, a replacement diskette will be provided to you for a nominal fee of $5.00 (send check or money order only). *This card must be totally filled out and accompanied by the defective diskette, a copy of the dated sales receipt, and a $5.00 check or money order made payable to Simon & Schuster, Inc.*

NAME ______________________ PHONE NUMBER (   ) ______________

ADDRESS ____

CITY ______________________ STATE ____________ ZIP ____________

PURCHASE DATE ______________________ PURCHASE PRICE ______________

Please send all requests to: MicroService Customer Service, Simon & Schuster/Prentice Hall Press, 200 Old Tappan Road, Old Tappan, NJ 07675
ATTN: Replacements.
NOTE: Simon & Schuster reserves the right, at its option, to refund your purchase price in lieu of providing a replacement diskette.

0-13-387705-1

Hewlett-Packard Laser Printer Power Pack
LIMITED WARRANTY REGISTRATION CARD

In order to preserve your rights as provided in the limited warranty, this card must be on file with Simon & Schuster within thirty days of purchase.

Please fill in the information requested:

NAME ______________________ PHONE NUMBER (   ) ______________

ADDRESS ____

CITY ______________________ STATE ____________ ZIP ____________

COMPUTER BRAND & MODEL ____________ DOS VERSION ____________ MEMORY ____________ K

Where did you purchase this product?

DEALER NAME? ______________________ PHONE NUMBER (   ) ______________

ADDRESS ____

CITY ______________________ STATE ____________ ZIP ____________

PURCHASE DATE ______________________ PURCHASE PRICE ______________

How did you learn about this product? (Check as many as applicable.)

STORE DISPLAY ________ SALESPERSON ________ MAGAZINE ARTICLE ________ ADVERTISEMENT ________

OTHER (Please explain) ____

How long have you owned or used this computer?

LESS THAN 30 DAYS ________ LESS THAN 6 MONTHS ________ 6 MONTHS TO A YEAR ________ OVER 1 YEAR ________

What is your primary use for the computer?

BUSINESS ________ PERSONAL ________ EDUCATION ________ OTHER (Please explain) ______________

Where is your computer located?

HOME ________ OFFICE ________ SCHOOL ________ OTHER (Please explain) ______________

67-38770

PUT
FIRST
CLASS
STAMP
HERE

Simon & Schuster, Inc.
Brady Books
15 Columbus Circle
New York, New York 10023

ATTN: **PRODUCT REGISTRATION**